D0677805

Oracle PL/SQL Built-ins
Pocket Reference

This belongs to

Oracle PL/SQL Built-ins
Pocket Reference

Steven Feuerstein,
John Beresniewicz & Chip Dawes

O'REILLY™

Beijing   Cambridge   Köln   Paris   Sebastopol   Taipei   Tokyo

Oracle PL/SQL Built-ins Pocket Reference

by Steven Feuerstein, John Beresniewicz, and Chip Dawes

Copyright © 1998 O'Reilly & Associates, Inc. All rights reserved.
Printed in the United States of America.
Published by O'Reilly & Associates, Inc., 101 Morris Street,
Sebastopol, CA 95472.

Editors: Deborah Russell and Gigi Estabrook

Production Editor: Jane Ellin

Cover Design: Edie Freedman

Printing History:

       October 1998:   First Edition.

ISBN: 1-56592-456-8

Table of Contents

Oracle PL/SQL Built-ins Pocket Reference

Introduction

The *Oracle PL/SQL Built-ins Pocket Reference* is a quick reference guide to the many built-in packages and functions
provided by Oracle Corporation. It contains a concise description of the syntax for the following:

- Built-in packages

- Built-in functions

- RESTRICT REFERENCES pragmas for the built-in packages

- Nonprogram elements (e.g., constants, exceptions, etc.)
  defined in the built-in packages

Although we don't include every single package and function
in this pocket reference, we've included all the built-ins that
most PL/SQL developers will ever need to use.

NOTE

Where a package, program, or function is supported only
for a particular version of Oracle (e.g., Oracle8), we indi-
cate this in the text.

The purpose of this pocket reference is to help PL/SQL users
find the syntax of specific built-in headers. It is not a self-
contained user guide; basic knowledge of PL/SQL and its

built-ins is required. For more information, see the following books:

Oracle PL/SQL Programming, by Steven Feuerstein and Bill Pribyl (O'Reilly & Associates, Second Edition, 1997).

Oracle Built-in Packages, by Steven Feuerstein, Charles Dye, and John Beresniewicz (O'Reilly & Associates, 1998).

Conventions

UPPERCASE
   Indicates PL/SQL keywords.

lowercase
   Indicates user-defined items such as parameters.

italic
   Indicates parameters within text.

[ ]
   In syntax descriptions, items in square brackets are optional.

Built-in Packages

PL/SQL packages allow you to collect related program elements and control access to those elements. Oracle provides a rich set of built-in packages that extend the functionality of PL/SQL in many important ways. Many of the built-ins allow you access to features that would otherwise be unavailable to you. You will find these packages helpful in developing applications, managing server-side resources, and performing many other operations.

The built-in packages are listed in this section in alphabetical order. For each package, we've shown the header (calling sequence) for each of the programs defined in the package, and provided a brief description of the program operation.

There are two default packages that deserve special mention. The STANDARD package contains many of the basic elements of the PL/SQL language (datatypes, functions, even basic operations like + and -). We describe the STANDARD functions later, in the "Built-in Functions" section.

The DBMS_STANDARD package, described in this section, contains kernel extensions to the STANDARD package.

DBMS_ALERT

DBMS_ALERT provides mechanisms for synchronous, transaction-based notification to multiple sessions that specific database events have occurred.

```
PROCEDURE DBMS_ALERT.REGISTER
    (name IN VARCHAR2);
```

Registers the calling session to receive notification of alert *name*.

```
PROCEDURE DBMS_ALERT.REMOVE
    (name IN VARCHAR2);
```

Unregisters the calling session from receiving notification of alert *name*.

```
PROCEDURE DBMS_ALERT.REMOVEALL;
```

Unregisters the calling session from notification of all alerts.

```
PROCEDURE DBMS_ALERT.SET_DEFAULTS
    (sensitivity IN NUMBER);
```

Defines configurable settings for the calling session. (*sensitivity* defines the loop interval sleep time in seconds.)

```
PROCEDURE DBMS_ALERT.SIGNAL
    (name IN VARCHAR2
    ,message IN VARCHAR2);
```

Signals the occurrence of alert *name* and attaches *message*. (Sessions registered for alert *name* are notified only when the signaling transaction commits.)

```
PROCEDURE DBMS_ALERT.WAITANY
    (name OUT VARCHAR2
    ,message OUT VARCHAR2
    ,status OUT INTEGER
    ,timeout IN NUMBER DEFAULT MAXWAIT);
```

Waits for up to *timeout* seconds to be notified of any alerts for which the session is registered. If *status* = 0 then *name* and *message* contain alert information. If *status* = 1 then *timeout* seconds elapsed without notification of any alert.

```
PROCEDURE DBMS_ALERT.WAITONE
    (name IN VARCHAR2
    ,message OUT VARCHAR2
    ,status OUT INTEGER
    ,timeout IN NUMBER DEFAULT MAXWAIT);
```

Waits for up to *timeout* seconds for notification of alert *name*. If *status* = 0 then *message* contains alert information. If *status* = 1 then *timeout* seconds elapsed without notification.

DBMS_APPLICATION_INFO

DBMS_APPLICATION_INFO allows applications to register their current execution status into several of the Oracle V$ virtual tables.

```
PROCEDURE DBMS_APPLICATION_INFO.READ_CLIENT_INFO
    (client_info OUT VARCHAR2);
```

Returns the currently registered *client_info* for the session.

```
PROCEDURE DBMS_APPLICATION_INFO.READ_MODULE
    (module_name OUT VARCHAR2
    ,action_name OUT VARCHAR2);
```

Returns the currently registered *module_name* and *action_name* for the session.

```
PROCEDURE DBMS_APPLICATION_INFO.SET_ACTION
    (action_name IN VARCHAR2);
```

Registers *action_name* into V$SESSION and V$SQLAREA as the current action for the session.

```
PROCEDURE DBMS_APPLICATION_INFO.SET_CLIENT_INFO
    (client_info IN VARCHAR2);
```

Registers *client_info* into V$SESSION as the current client information for the session.

```
PROCEDURE DBMS_APPLICATION_INFO.SET_MODULE
    (module_name IN VARCHAR2
    ,action_name IN VARCHAR2);
```

Registers *module_name* and *action_name* into V$SESSION and V$SQLAREA as the current module and action for the session.

```
PROCEDURE DBMS_APPLICATION_INFO.SET_SESSION_LONGOPS
    (hint IN OUT BINARY_INTEGER
    ,context IN NUMBER DEFAULT 0
    ,stepid IN NUMBER DEFAULT 0
    ,stepsofar IN NUMBER DEFAULT 0
    ,steptotal IN NUMBER DEFAULT 0
    ,sofar IN NUMBER DEFAULT 0
    ,totalwork IN NUMBER DEFAULT 0
    ,application_data_1 IN NUMBER DEFAULT 0
    ,application_data_2 IN NUMBER DEFAULT 0
    ,application_data_3 IN NUMBER DEFAULT 0);
```

Inserts or updates runtime data for long-running operations in the V$SESSION_LONGOPS virtual table. Rows are identified by the value of *hint*; a new row is acquired when *hint* is set to the package constant set_session_longops_nohint. Unique combinations of *context* and *stepid* also force a new row.

The SET_SESSION_LONGOPS procedure is used to track the progress of long-running operations by allowing the entry and modification of data in the V$SESSION_LONGOPS virtual table.

DBMS_AQ

The DBMS_AQ package allows you to enqueue to and dequeue messages from queues created in the Oracle Advanced Queuing facility. Oracle8 only.

```
PROCEDURE DBMS_AQ.ENQUEUE
    (queue_name IN VARCHAR2
    ,enqueue_options IN DBMS_AQ.ENQUEUE_OPTIONS_T
    ,message_properties IN DBMS_AQ.MESSAGE_PROPERTIES_T
    ,payload IN payload_type
    ,msgid OUT RAW);
```

Adds the message *payload* to the queue *queue_name*, using the options specified by the *enqueue_options* record. The *payload_type* is either RAW or the name of an object TYPE. Returns the pointer to the message in *msgid*.

```
PROCEDURE DBMS_AQ.DEQUEUE
    (queue_name IN VARCHAR2
    ,dequeue_options IN DBMS_AQ.DEQUEUE_OPTIONS_T
    ,message_properties OUT DBMS_AQ.MESSAGE_PROPERTIES_T
    ,payload OUT <payload_type>
    ,msgid OUT RAW);
```

Retrieves the message *payload* (either a RAW or an object of the specified TYPE) with *message_properties* specified by the *dequeue_options*. Also returns the *msgid* of that message.

DBMS_AQADM

The DBMS_AQADM package provides a set of programs you can use to create, manage, and drop queues and queue tables in the Oracle Advanced Queuing facility.

```
PROCEDURE DBMS_AQADM.CREATE_QUEUE_TABLE
    (queue_table IN VARCHAR2
    ,queue_payload_type IN VARCHAR2
    ,storage_clause IN VARCHAR2 DEFAULT NULL
    ,sort_list IN VARCHAR2 DEFAULT NULL
    ,multiple_consumers IN BOOLEAN DEFAULT FALSE
    ,message_grouping IN BINARY_INTEGER DEFAULT NONE
    ,comment IN VARCHAR2 DEFAULT NULL
    ,auto_commit IN BOOLEAN DEFAULT TRUE);
```

Creates a queue table named *queue_table* of *queue_payload_type* (RAW or the name of an object TYPE).

```
PROCEDURE DBMS_AQADM.CREATE_QUEUE
    (queue_name IN VARCHAR2
    ,queue_table IN VARCHAR2
    ,queue_type IN BINARY_INTEGER DEFAULT NORMAL_QUEUE
    ,max_retries IN NUMBER DEFAULT 0
    ,retry_delay IN NUMBER DEFAULT 0
    ,retention_time IN NUMBER DEFAULT 0
    ,dependency_tracking IN BOOLEAN DEFAULT FALSE
    ,comment IN VARCHAR2 DEFAULT NULL
    ,auto_commit IN BOOLEAN DEFAULT TRUE);
```

Creates a queue named *queue_name* in the queue table *queue_table*.

```
PROCEDURE DBMS_AQADM.DROP_QUEUE
    (queue_name IN VARCHAR2
    ,auto_commit IN BOOLEAN DEFAULT TRUE);
```

Drops the *queue_name* queue.

```
PROCEDURE DBMS_AQADM.DROP_QUEUE_TABLE
    (queue_table IN VARCHAR2
    ,force IN BOOLEAN DEFAULT FALSE
    ,auto_commit IN BOOLEAN DEFAULT TRUE);
```

Drops the *queue_name* queue from the queue table *queue_table*.

```
PROCEDURE DBMS_AQADM.START_QUEUE
    (queue_name IN VARCHAR2
    ,enqueue IN BOOLEAN DEFAULT TRUE
    ,dequeue IN BOOLEAN DEFAULT TRUE);
```

Starts the *queue_name* queue with *enqueue* and/or *dequeue* capabilities.

```
PROCEDURE DBMS_AQADM.STOP_QUEUE
    (queue_name IN VARCHAR2
    ,enqueue IN BOOLEAN DEFAULT TRUE
    ,dequeue IN BOOLEAN DEFAULT TRUE
    ,wait IN BOOLEAN DEFAULT TRUE);
```

Stops the *queue_name* queue for *enqueue* and/or *dequeue* capabilities with/without waiting for completion of outstanding transactions.

```
PROCEDURE DBMS_AQADM.ALTER_QUEUE
    (queue_name IN VARCHAR2
    ,max_retries IN NUMBER DEFAULT NULL
    ,retry_delay IN NUMBER DEFAULT NULL
    ,retention_time IN NUMBER DEFAULT NULL
    ,auto_commit IN BOOLEAN DEFAULT TRUE);
```

Alters the specified characteristics of the *queue_name* queue.

```
PROCEDURE DBMS_AQADM.ADD_SUBSCRIBER
    (queue_name IN VARCHAR2
    ,subscriber IN SYS.AQ$_AGENT);
```

Adds the *subscriber* agent to the *queue_name* queue.

```
PROCEDURE DBMS_AQADM.REMOVE_SUBSCRIBER
    (queue_name IN VARCHAR2
    ,subscriber IN SYS.AQ$_AGENT);
```

Removes the *subscriber* agent from the *queue_name* queue.

```
PROCEDURE DBMS_AQADM.GRANT_TYPE_ACCESS
    (user_name IN VARCHAR2);
```

Grants to *user_name* the ability to create queues that work with multiple consumers.

```
FUNCTION DBMS_AQADM.QUEUE_SUBSCRIBERS
    (queue_name IN VARCHAR2)
RETURN AQ$_SUBSCRIBER_LIST_T;
```

Returns the list of subscribers for the *queue_name* queue.

```
PROCEDURE DBMS_AQADM.START_TIME_MANAGER;
```

Starts the Queue Monitor process.

```
PROCEDURE DBMS_AQADM.STOP_TIME_MANAGER;
```

Stops the Queue Monitor process.

DBMS_DDL

DBMS_DDL contains programs to recompile stored code, analyze and compute statistics for database objects, and modify the referenceability of object identifiers in Oracle8.

```
PROCEDURE DBMS_DDL.ALTER_COMPILE
    (type IN VARCHAR2
    ,schema IN VARCHAR2
    ,name IN VARCHAR2);
```

Recompiles the stored PL/SQL object *name* (case-sensitive) owned by *schema* of type *type*. NULL *schema* uses current schema. Valid values for type are PROCEDURE, FUNCTION, PACKAGE, PACKAGE BODY, and PACKAGE SPECIFICATION.

```
PROCEDURE DBMS_DDL.ALTER_TABLE_NOT_REFERENCEABLE
    (table_name IN VARCHAR2
    ,table_schema IN VARCHAR2 DEFAULT NULL
    ,affected_schema IN VARCHAR2 DEFAULT NULL);
```

Reverts references to object *table_name* by schema *affected_schema* from *table_name* owned by *table_schema* to the default. Oracle8 only.

```
PROCEDURE DBMS_DDL.ALTER_TABLE_REFERENCEABLE
    (table_name IN VARCHAR2
    ,table_schema IN VARCHAR2 DEFAULT NULL
    ,affected_schema IN VARCHAR2 DEFAULT NULL);
```

Makes the object table owned by *table_schema* the table
referenced from schema *affected_schema* for object name
table_name. Oracle8 only.

```
PROCEDURE DBMS_DDL.ANALYZE_OBJECT
    (type IN VARCHAR2
    ,schema IN VARCHAR2
    ,name IN VARCHAR2
    ,method IN VARCHAR2
    ,estimate_rows IN NUMBER DEFAULT NULL
    ,estimate_percent IN NUMBER DEFAULT NULL
    ,method_opt IN VARCHAR2 DEFAULT NULL);
```

Analyzes database object *name* owned by *schema* of type
type (TABLE, INDEX, or CLUSTER) using option *method*
(ESTIMATE, NULL, or DELETE). When *method* is ESTI-
MATE, either *estimate_rows* or *estimate_percent* must be
specified to identify sample size. Additional analyze
options specifiable by *method_opt* are FOR TABLE, FOR
ALL COLUMNS [SIZE *N*], FOR ALL INDEXED COLUMNS
[SIZE *N*], and FOR ALL INDEXES.

DBMS_DESCRIBE

The DBMS_DESCRIBE package contains a single procedure
used to describe the arguments of a stored PL/SQL procedure
or function.

```
PROCEDURE DBMS_DESCRIBE.DESCRIBE_PROCEDURE
    (object_name IN VARCHAR2
    ,reserved1 IN VARCHAR2
    ,reserved2 IN VARCHAR2
    ,overload OUT DBMS_DESCRIBE.NUMBER_TABLE
    ,position OUT DBMS_DESCRIBE.NUMBER_TABLE
    ,level OUT DBMS_DESCRIBE.NUMBER_TABLE
    ,argument_name OUT DBMS_DESCRIBE.VARCHAR2_TABLE
    ,datatype OUT DBMS_DESCRIBE.NUMBER_TABLE
    ,default_value OUT DBMS_DESCRIBE.NUMBER_TABLE
    ,in_out OUT DBMS_DESCRIBE.NUMBER_TABLE
    ,length OUT DBMS_DESCRIBE.NUMBER_TABLE
    ,precision OUT DBMS_DESCRIBE.NUMBER_TABLE
    ,scale OUT DBMS_DESCRIBE.NUMBER_TABLE
    ,radix OUT DBMS_DESCRIBE.NUMBER_TABLE
    ,spare OUT DBMS_DESCRIBE.NUMBER_TABLE);
```

Returns information about the parameters and RETURN
type (if a function) of the specified object (procedure or

---

function) in a set of PL/SQL tables, whose types are described in the same package.

DBMS_JOB

DBMS_JOB is an interface into the Oracle job queue subsystem that allows automated, unattended scheduling and execution of PL/SQL programs.

```
PROCEDURE DBMS_JOB.BROKEN
    (job IN BINARY_INTEGER
    ,broken IN BOOLEAN
    ,next_date IN DATE DEFAULT SYSDATE);
```

Sets or unsets the Boolean *broken* flag for the *job*, and optionally sets the next execution date specified by *next_date*. Jobs flagged with *broken* = TRUE are not automatically executed.

```
PROCEDURE DBMS_JOB.CHANGE
    (job IN BINARY_INTEGER
    ,what IN VARCHAR2
    ,next_date IN DATE
    ,interval IN VARCHAR2);
```

Changes one or more of the parameters *what, next_date*, or *interval* for *job*.

```
PROCEDURE DBMS_JOB.INTERVAL
    (job IN BINARY_INTEGER
    ,interval IN VARCHAR2);
```

Changes the date expression used to determine the next execution date for *job* to *interval*.

```
PROCEDURE DBMS_JOB.ISUBMIT
    (job IN BINARY_INTEGER
    ,what IN VARCHAR2
    ,next_date IN VARCHAR2
    ,interval IN VARCHAR2 DEFAULT 'null'
    ,no_parse IN BOOLEAN DEFAULT FALSE);
```

Submits a job with the specified *job* number and PL/SQL definition *what*, scheduled to execute at *next_date* and every *interval* thereafter. When *no_parse* is TRUE, parsing of the PL/SQL in *what* is deferred until execution.

```
PROCEDURE DBMS_JOB.NEXT_DATE
    (job IN BINARY_INTEGER
    ,next_date IN DATE);
```

Changes the next scheduled date of execution for *job* to
next_date.

```
PROCEDURE DBMS_JOB.REMOVE
    (job IN BINARY_INTEGER);
```

Removes *job* from the *job* queue. If *job* is currently
executing, it will run to normal completion, but will not be
rescheduled.

```
PROCEDURE DBMS_JOB.RUN
    (job IN BINARY_INTEGER);
```

Immediately executes *job* in the current session.

```
PROCEDURE DBMS_JOB.SUBMIT
    (job OUT BINARY_INTEGER
    ,what IN VARCHAR2
    ,next_date IN DATE DEFAULT SYSDATE
    ,interval IN VARCHAR2 DEFAULT 'null'
    ,no_parse IN BOOLEAN DEFAULT FALSE);
```

Submits a job to the job queue with PL/SQL definition
what, scheduled to execute at *next_date* and every
interval thereafter. *Job* returns the identification number for
the job. When *no_parse* is TRUE, parsing of the PL/SQL in
what is deferred until execution.

```
PROCEDURE DBMS_JOB.USER_EXPORT
    (job IN BINARY_INTEGER
    ,mycall IN OUT VARCHAR2);
```

Returns a character string in *mycall* containing a call to
DBMS_JOB.ISUBMIT that can be used to re-submit *job* to
the job queue.

```
PROCEDURE DBMS_JOB.WHAT
    (job IN BINARY_INTEGER
    ,what IN VARCHAR2);
```

Changes the PL/SQL definition for *job* to *what*.

DBMS_LOB

DBMS_LOB provides a mechanism for accessing and manipulating large objects. LOBs include BLOBs (binary large

---

objects), CLOBs (character large objects), NCLOBs (National
Language Support character large objects), and BFILEs (binary
files). The CHARACTER SET ANY_CS clauses in the CLOB
declarations allow either CLOB or NCLOB locators. Oracle 8
only.

```
PROCEDURE DBMS_LOB.APPEND
    (dest_lob IN OUT BLOB
    ,src_lob  IN BLOB);
```

```
PROCEDURE DBMS_LOB.APPEND
    (dest_lob IN OUT CLOB CHARACTER SET ANY_CS
    ,src_lob IN CLOB CHARACTER SET dest_lob%CHARSET);
```

Appends the contents of the source LOB *src_lob* to the
destination LOB *dest_lob*. Both *src_lob* and *dest_lob* must
be of the same LOB type: BLOB, CLOB, or NCLOB.

```
FUNCTION DBMS_LOB.COMPARE
    (lob_1 IN BLOB | CLOB CHARACTER SET ANY_CS
    ,lob_2 IN BLOB | CLOB CHARACTER SET lob_1%CHARSET
    ,amount IN INTEGER := 4294967295
    ,offset_1 IN INTEGER := 1
    ,offset_2 IN INTEGER := 1)
RETURN INTEGER;
```

```
FUNCTION DBMS_LOB.COMPARE
    (file_1 IN BFILE
    ,file_2 IN BFILE
    ,amount IN INTEGER
    ,offset_1 IN INTEGER := 1
    ,offset_2 IN INTEGER := 1)
RETURN INTEGER;
```

Compares input LOBs *lob_1* and *lob_2* or *file_1* and *file_2*
across *amount* bytes, optionally starting the comparison
offset_1 and *offset_2* bytes into the input files. Both inputs
must be of the same LOB type: BLOB, CLOB, NCLOB, or
BFILE.

Returns 0 if they exactly match, non-0 if they don't match,
or NULL if any of *amount*, *offset_1*, or *offset_2* are either
less than 1 or greater than lobmaxsize.

```
PROCEDURE DBMS_LOB.COPY
    (dest_lob IN OUT BLOB,
    ,src_lob IN BLOB
```

```
    ,amount IN INTEGER
    ,dest_offset IN INTEGER := 1
    ,src_offset IN INTEGER := 1);

PROCEDURE DBMS_LOB.COPY
    (dest_lob IN OUT CLOB CHARACTER SET ANY_CS
    ,src_lob IN CLOB CHARACTER SET dest_lob%CHARSET,
    ,amount IN INTEGER
    ,dest_offset IN INTEGER := 1
    ,src_offset IN INTEGER := 1);
```

Copies *amount* bytes (BLOB) or characters (CLOB) from source LOB *lob_loc*, starting *src_offset* bytes or characters into the source LOB to the destination (target) LOB, *dest_lob*, starting *dest_offset* into the destination LOB. Both *src_lob* and *dest_lob* must be the same LOB type: BLOB, CLOB, or NCLOB.

```
PROCEDURE DBMS_LOB.ERASE
    (lob_loc IN OUT BLOB | CLOB CHARACTER SET ANY_CS
    ,amount IN OUT INTEGER
    ,offset IN INTEGER := 1);
```

Erases (zero byte fill) *amount* bytes (BLOB) or characters (CLOB) in the LOB *lob_loc*, beginning *offset* bytes or characters into the LOB *lob_loc*.

```
PROCEDURE DBMS_LOB.FILECLOSE
    (file_loc IN OUT BFILE);
```

Closes the BFILE *file_loc*, whether it is open or not.

```
PROCEDURE DBMS_LOB.FILECLOSEALL;
```

Closes all open BFILEs in the current session.

```
FUNCTION DBMS_LOB.FILEEXISTS
    (file_loc IN BFILE)
RETURN INTEGER;
```

Returns 1 if BFILE *file_loc* exists; returns 0 otherwise.

```
PROCEDURE DBMS_LOB.FILEGETNAME
    (file_loc IN BFILE
    ,dir_alias OUT VARCHAR2
    ,filename OUT VARCHAR2);
```

Gets directory alias (as previously defined via the CREATE DIRECTORY command) and filename for the given file locator *file_loc*.

```
FUNCTION DBMS_LOB.FILEISOPEN
    (file_loc IN BFILE)
RETURN INTEGER;
```

Returns 1 if the BFILE *file_loc* is open; returns 0 otherwise.

```
PROCEDURE DBMS_LOB.FILEOPEN
    (file_loc IN OUT BFILE
    ,open_mode IN BINARY_INTEGER := FILE_READONLY);
```

Opens BFILE *file_loc* for read-only access.

```
FUNCTION DBMS_LOB.GETLENGTH
    (lob_loc IN BLOB)
RETURN INTEGER;
```

```
FUNCTION DBMS_LOB.GETLENGTH
    (lob_loc IN CLOB CHARACTER SET ANY_CS)
RETURN INTEGER;
```

```
FUNCTION DBMS_LOB.GETLENGTH
    (lob_loc IN BFILE)
RETURN INTEGER;
```

Returns the size in bytes or characters of the LOB *lob_loc*.

```
FUNCTION DBMS_LOB.INSTR
    (lob_loc IN BLOB | BFILE
    ,pattern IN RAW
    ,offset IN INTEGER := 1
    ,nth IN INTEGER := 1)
RETURN INTEGER;
```

```
FUNCTION DBMS_LOB.INSTR
    (lob_loc IN CLOB CHARACTER SET ANY_CS
    ,pattern IN VARCHAR2 CHARACTER SET lob_loc%CHARSET
    ,offset IN INTEGER := 1
    ,nth IN INTEGER := 1)
RETURN INTEGER;
```

Similar to the built-in function INSTR. Returns the byte (BLOB) or character (CLOB) offset in LOB *lob_loc* where the *nth* occurrence of *pattern* is found. The search begins *offset* bytes or characters into *lob_loc*.

```
PROCEDURE DBMS_LOB.LOADFROMFILE
    (dest_lob IN OUT BLOB | CLOB CHARACTER SET ANY_CS
    ,src_lob IN BFILE
    ,amount IN INTEGER
```

```
    ,dest_offset IN INTEGER := 1
    ,src_offset IN INTEGER := 1);
```

Copies *amount* bytes of data from the source BFILE *src_lob* to the destination (target) LOB *dest_lob*, starting *src_offset* bytes into the source BFILE and *dest_offset* bytes into the destination (target) LOB.

```
PROCEDURE DBMS_LOB.READ
    (lob_loc IN BLOB | BFILE
    ,amount IN OUT BINARY_INTEGER
    ,offset IN INTEGER
    ,buffer OUT RAW);

PROCEDURE DBMS_LOB.READ
    (lob_loc IN CLOB CHARACTER SET ANY_CS
    ,amount IN OUT BINARY_INTEGER
    ,offset IN INTEGER
    ,buffer OUT VARCHAR2 CHARACTER SET lob_loc%CHARSET);
```

Copies *amount* bytes (BLOB) or characters (CLOB) from source LOB *lob_loc*, starting *offset* bytes or characters into the LOB to the destination (target) variable, *buffer*. Returns the actual number of bytes or characters copied in *amount*.

```
FUNCTION DBMS_LOB.SUBSTR
    (lob_loc IN BLOB | BFILE
    ,amount IN INTEGER := 32767
    ,offset IN INTEGER := 1)
RETURN RAW;

FUNCTION DBMS_LOB.SUBSTR
    (lob_loc IN CLOB CHARACTER SET ANY_CS
    ,amount IN INTEGER := 32767
    ,offset IN INTEGER := 1)
RETURN VARCHAR2 CHARACTER SET lob_loc%CHARSET;
```

Similar to the built-in function SUBSTR. Returns *amount* bytes (BLOB) or characters (CLOB) of the LOB *lob_loc* starting *offset* bytes or characters into the LOB.

```
PROCEDURE DBMS_LOB.TRIM
    (lob_loc IN OUT BLOB | CLOB CHARACTER SET ANY_CS
    ,newlen IN INTEGER);
```

Truncates the LOB *lob_loc* to *newlen* bytes (BLOB) or characters (CLOB).

```
PROCEDURE DBMS_LOB.WRITE
    (lob_loc IN OUT BLOB
    ,amount IN BINARY_INTEGER
    ,offset IN INTEGER
    ,buffer IN RAW);

PROCEDURE DBMS_LOB.WRITE
    (lob_loc IN OUT CLOB CHARACTER SET ANY_CS
    ,amount IN BINARY_INTEGER
    ,offset IN INTEGER
    ,buffer IN VARCHAR2 CHARACTER SET lob_loc%CHARSET);
```

Copies *amount* bytes from source variable *buffer* to the destination LOB *lob_loc*, starting *offset* bytes (BLOB) or characters (CLOB) into the LOB, overwriting any existing data in *lob_loc*.

DBMS_LOCK

DBMS_LOCK makes Oracle lock management services available for implementation of specialized, non-data locking and serialization requirements within applications.

```
PROCEDURE DBMS_LOCK.ALLOCATE_UNIQUE
    (lockname IN VARCHAR2
    ,lockhandle OUT VARCHAR2
    ,expiration_secs IN INTEGER DEFAULT 864000);
```

Allocates a unique *lockhandle* for the lock identified by *lockname* to last for *expiration_secs* seconds. Also performs a COMMIT.

```
FUNCTION DBMS_LOCK.CONVERT
    (id IN INTEGER | lockhandle IN VARCHAR2
    ,lockmode IN INTEGER
    ,timeout IN NUMBER DEFAULT MAXWAIT)
RETURN INTEGER;
```

Converts the lock identified by either *id* or *lockhandle* to the mode specified by *lockmode*, waiting for up to *timeout* seconds for successful completion. *lockmode* must be a valid constant as defined in the DBMS_LOCK package. Return values are 0 = success; 1 = timed out; 2 = deadlock; 3 = parameter error; 4 = do not own lock, cannot convert; or 5 = illegal lockhandle.

```
FUNCTION DBMS_LOCK.RELEASE
    (id IN INTEGER | lockhandle IN VARCHAR2)
RETURN INTEGER;
```

Releases the lock identified by either *id* or *lockhandle*.
Return values are: 0 = success; 3 = parameter error; 4 = do
not own lock, cannot release; or 5 = illegal lockhandle.

```
FUNCTION DBMS_LOCK.REQUEST
    (id IN INTEGER | lockhandle IN VARCHAR2
    ,lockmode IN INTEGER DEFAULT X_MODE
    ,timeout IN INTEGER DEFAULT MAXWAIT
    ,release_on_commit IN BOOLEAN DEFAULT FALSE)
RETURN INTEGER;
```

Acquires the lock identified by either *id* or *lockhandle* in
the mode specified by *lockmode*, waiting for up to *timeout*
seconds for successful completion. When *release_on_
commit* is TRUE, the lock is automatically released by
transaction COMMIT or ROLLBACK. *lockmode* must be a
valid constant as defined in the DBMS_LOCK package.
Return values are 0 = success; 1 = timed out; 2 = deadlock; 3 = parameter error; 4 = do not own lock, cannot
convert; or 5 = illegal lockhandle.

```
PROCEDURE DBMS_LOCK.SLEEP
    (seconds IN NUMBER);
```

Suspends the session for *seconds* seconds.

DBMS_OUTPUT

This package provides a mechanism for displaying information on your session's output device from within a PL/SQL
program. You can use it as a crude debugger or trace facility.

```
PROCEDURE DBMS_OUTPUT.DISABLE;
```

Disables output from the package and purges the DBMS_
OUTPUT buffer.

```
PROCEDURE DBMS_OUTPUT.ENABLE
    (buffer_size IN INTEGER DEFAULT 20000);
```

Enables output from the package and sets to *buffer_size*
the maximum number of bytes that can be stored in the
buffer.

```
PROCEDURE DBMS_OUTPUT.GET_LINE
    (line OUT VARCHAR2
    ,status OUT INTEGER);
```

Gets the next line from the buffer and places it in *line*. A *status* of 0 means successful retrieval; 1 means failure.

```
PROCEDURE DBMS_OUTPUT.GET_LINES
    (lines OUT DBMS_OUTPUT.CHARARR
    ,numlines IN OUT INTEGER);
```

Gets *numlines* number of lines from the buffer and places them in the *lines* PL/SQL table.

```
PROCEDURE DBMS_OUTPUT.NEW_LINE;
```

Writes a newline character to the DBMS_OUTPUT buffer.

```
PROCEDURE DBMS_OUTPUT.PUT
    (a IN DATE|NUMBER|VARCHAR2);
```

Puts the data contained in *a* in the DBMS_OUTPUT buffer and does not append a newline character.

```
PROCEDURE DBMS_OUTPUT.PUT_LINE
    (a IN DATE|NUMBER|VARCHAR2);
```

Puts the data contained in *a* in the DBMS_OUTPUT buffer and then appends a newline character.

DBMS_PIPE

DBMS_PIPE permits communication of messages between database sessions using memory-based structures. Communication is asynchronous, non-transactional, and persists beyond session lifetime.

```
FUNCTION DBMS_PIPE.CREATE_PIPE
    (pipename IN VARCHAR2
    ,maxpipesize IN INTEGER DEFAULT 8192
    ,private IN BOOLEAN DEFAULT TRUE)
RETURN INTEGER;
```

Creates a pipe identified by *pipename* with maximum size *maxpipesize* and returns 0. When *private* is FALSE, the pipe is publicly accessible.

```
FUNCTION DBMS_PIPE.NEXT_ITEM_TYPE
RETURN INTEGER;
```

Returns an integer identifying the datatype of the next item in the session message buffer.

```
PROCEDURE DBMS_PIPE.PACK_MESSAGE
    (item IN VARCHAR2 | NUMBER | DATE);
```

Packs *item* into the session message buffer, overloaded on the datatype of *item*.

```
PROCEDURE DBMS_PIPE.PACK_MESSAGE_RAW
    (item IN RAW);
```

Packs the raw data in *item* into the session message buffer.

```
PROCEDURE DBMS_PIPE.PACK_MESSAGE_ROWID
    (item IN ROWID);
```

Packs the ROWID data in *item* into the session message buffer.

```
PROCEDURE DBMS_PIPE.PURGE
    (pipename IN VARCHAR2);
```

Purges all messages from *pipename*.

```
FUNCTION DBMS_PIPE.RECEIVE_MESSAGE
    (pipename IN VARCHAR2
    ,timeout IN INTEGER DEFAULT MAXWAIT)
RETURN INTEGER;
```

Receives a message from *pipename* into the session message buffer, waiting for up to *timeout* seconds for successful completion. Returns 0 for success and 1 for timeout.

```
FUNCTION DBMS_PIPE.REMOVE_PIPE
    (pipename IN VARCHAR2)
RETURN INTEGER;
```

Removes *pipename* and frees its memory back to the shared pool, returning 0.

```
PROCEDURE DBMS_PIPE.RESET_BUFFER;
```

Resets the session message buffer's pack and unpack indicators, effectively discarding all contents.

```
FUNCTION DBMS_PIPE.SEND_MESSAGE
    (pipename IN VARCHAR2
    ,timeout IN INTEGER DEFAULT MAXWAIT
    ,maxpipesize IN INTEGER DEFAULT 8192)
RETURN INTEGER;
```

Sends the contents of the session message buffer onto *pipename*, waiting for up to *timeout* seconds for successful

---

completion and optionally increasing the maximum size of
pipename to *maxpipesize*. Returns 0 for success and 1 for
timeout.

```
FUNCTION DBMS_PIPE.UNIQUE_SESSION_NAME
RETURN VARCHAR2;
```

Returns a string identifier unique to the session up to 30
bytes in length.

```
PROCEDURE DBMS_PIPE.UNPACK_MESSAGE
    (item OUT VARCHAR2 | NUMBER | DATE);
```

Unpacks the next data item in the message buffer into
item, overloaded on the datatype of *item*.

```
PROCEDURE DBMS_PIPE.UNPACK_MESSAGE_RAW
    (item OUT RAW);
```

Unpacks the next data item in the message buffer into *item*
when it is of datatype RAW.

```
PROCEDURE DBMS_PIPE.UNPACK_MESSAGE_ROWID
    (item OUT ROWID);
```

Unpacks the next data item in the message buffer into *item*
when it is of datatype ROWID.

DBMS_RANDOM

DBMS_RANDOM provides a random number generating
utility. Oracle8 only.

```
PROCEDURE DBMS_RANDOM.INITIALIZE
    (seed IN BINARY_INTEGER);
```

Initializes the random number generator with the value of
seed, which should be at least five digits in length.

```
FUNCTION DBMS_RANDOM.RANDOM
RETURN BINARY_INTEGER;
```

Returns a random integer value from the random number
generator.

```
PROCEDURE DBMS_RANDOM.SEED
    (seed IN BINARY_INTEGER);
```

Changes the random number generator's seed value to
seed, which should be at least five digits in length.

```
PROCEDURE DBMS_RANDOM.TERMINATE;
```
Releases resources used by the random number generator when no longer needed.

DBMS_ROWID

DBMS_ROWID provides routines for working with ROWIDs. ROWIDs changed structure in Oracle8, and for Oracle8 this built-in works with both the old and new ROWID types.

An Oracle7 (restricted) ROWID has three parts in base 16 (hex):

BBBBBBBB.RRRR.FFFF

An Oracle8 (extended) ROWID has four parts in base 64:

OOOOOOFFFBBBBBBBRRR

where:

OOOOOO is the object number.
FFFF (FFF) is the absolute (V7) or relative (V8) file number.
BBBBBBBB (BBBBB) is the block number within the file.
RRRR (RRR) is the row number within the block.

```
FUNCTION DBMS_ROWID.ROWID_BLOCK_NUMBER
    (row_id IN ROWID)
RETURN NUMBER;
```
Returns the block number component of *row_id*.

```
FUNCTION DBMS_ROWID.ROWID_CREATE
    (rowid_type IN NUMBER
    ,object_number IN NUMBER
    ,relative_fno IN NUMBER
    ,block_number IN NUMBER
    ,row_number IN NUMBER)
RETURN ROWID;
```
Creates a *rowid_type* ROWID composed of *object_number*, *relative_fno, block_number*, and *row_number* ROWID. *rowid_type* can be ROWID_TYPE_EXTENDED or ROWID_TYPE_RESTRICTED. *object_number* can be ROWID_OBJECT_UNDEFINED or the object number (OID).

```
PROCEDURE DBMS_ROWID.ROWID_INFO
    (rowid_in IN ROWID
```

```
,rowid_type OUT NUMBER
,object_number OUT NUMBER
,relative_fno OUT NUMBER
,block_number OUT NUMBER
,row_number OUT NUMBER);
```

Parses *rowid_in* into its individual components. *rowid_type* can be ROWID_TYPE_EXTENDED or ROWID_TYPE_RESTRICTED. *object_number* can be ROWID_OBJECT_UNDEFINED or the object number (OID).

```
FUNCTION DBMS_ROWID.ROWID_OBJECT
    (row_id IN ROWID)
RETURN NUMBER;
```

Returns the object number component of *row_id*.

```
FUNCTION DBMS_ROWID.ROWID_RELATIVE_FNO
    (row_id IN ROWID)
RETURN NUMBER;
```

Returns the relative file number component of *row_id*.

```
FUNCTION DBMS_ROWID.ROWID_ROW_NUMBER
    (row_id IN ROWID)
RETURN NUMBER;
```

Returns the row number component of *row_id*.

```
FUNCTION DBMS_ROWID.ROWID_TO_ABSOLUTE_FNO
    (row_id IN ROWID
    ,schema_name IN VARCHAR2
    ,object_name IN VARCHAR2)
RETURN NUMBER;
```

Returns the absolute file number for *row_id, schema_name*, and *object_name*.

```
FUNCTION DBMS_ROWID.ROWID_TO_EXTENDED
    (old_rowid IN ROWID
    ,schema_name IN VARCHAR2
    ,object_name IN VARCHAR2
    ,conversion_type IN INTEGER)
RETURN ROWID;
```

Returns the extended ROWID for the restricted *old_rowid, schema_name*, and *object_name* using *conversion_type*. The *conversion_type* can be either ROWID_CONVERT_INTERNAL (ROWID was stored in a column of type ROWID) or ROWID_CONVERT_EXTERNAL (ROWID was stored in a column of type CHAR/VARCHAR/VARCHAR2).

```
FUNCTION DBMS_ROWID.ROWID_TO_RESTRICTED
    (old_rowid IN ROWID
    ,conversion_type IN INTEGER)
RETURN ROWID;
```

Returns a restricted ROWID for the extended *old_rowid* using *conversion_type*. The *conversion_type* can be either ROWID_CONVERT_INTERNAL (ROWID will be stored in a column of type ROWID) or ROWID_CONVERT_EXTERNAL (ROWID will be stored in a column of type CHAR/VARCHAR/VARCHAR2).

```
FUNCTION DBMS_ROWID.ROWID_TYPE
    (row_id IN ROWID)
RETURN NUMBER;
```

Returns ROWID_TYPE_EXTENDED or ROWID_TYPE_RESTRICTED for *row_id*.

```
FUNCTION DBMS_ROWID.ROWID_VERIFY
    (rowid_in IN ROWID
    ,schema_name IN VARCHAR2
    ,object_name IN VARCHAR2
    ,conversion_type IN INTEGER)
RETURN NUMBER;
```

Returns ROWID_VALID or ROWID_INVALID for *rowid_in*, *schema_name*, and *object_name*, using *conversion_type*. The *conversion_type* can be either ROWID_CONVERT_INTERNAL (*rowid_in* is stored in a column of type ROWID) or ROWID_CONVERT_EXTERNAL (*rowid_in* is stored in a column of type CHAR/VARCHAR/VARCHAR2).

DBMS_SESSION

DBMS_SESSION provides facilities to set and modify session settings, enable or disable roles, and manage session resources.

```
PROCEDURE DBMS_SESSION.CLOSE_DATABASE_LINK
    (dblink IN VARCHAR2);
```

Closes the database link *dblink* or raises an exception if *dblink* is not open or is in use.

```
PROCEDURE DBMS_SESSION.FREE_UNUSED_USER_MEMORY;
```

Releases freeable session memory back to the operating system (dedicated connection) or the Oracle shared pool (shared server connection).

```
FUNCTION DBMS_SESSION.IS_ROLE_ENABLED
    (rolename IN VARCHAR2)
RETURN BOOLEAN;
```

Returns TRUE if the *rolename* is currently enabled in the session.

```
FUNCTION DBMS_SESSION.IS_SESSION_ALIVE
    (uniqueid IN VARCHAR2)
RETURN BOOLEAN;
```

Returns TRUE if the session identified by *uniqueid* is still alive. Oracle8 only.

```
PROCEDURE DBMS_SESSION.RESET_PACKAGE;
```

Resets all package states in the session, destroying the values of all persistent package variables.

```
PROCEDURE DBMS_SESSION.SET_CLOSE_CACHED_OPEN_CURSORS
    (close_cursors IN BOOLEAN);
```

Overrides the CLOSE_CACHED_OPEN_CURSORS database parameter at the session level with the value in *close_cursors*.

```
PROCEDURE DBMS_SESSION.SET_LABEL
    (lbl IN VARCHAR2);
```

Sets the session's Trusted Oracle session label to *lbl*.

```
PROCEDURE DBMS_SESSION.SET_MLS_LABEL_FORMAT
    (fmt IN VARCHAR2);
```

Sets the session's default Trusted Oracle label format to *fmt*.

```
PROCEDURE DBMS_SESSION.SET_NLS
    (param IN VARCHAR2
    ,value IN VARCHAR2);
```

Sets the National Language Support parameter *param* to *value*. When *value* is a format mask, use a triple-quoted string.

```
PROCEDURE DBMS_SESSION.SET_ROLE
    (role_cmd IN VARCHAR2);
```

Enables role(s) by appending *role_cmd* to the SET_ROLE command and executing. Disables all roles by setting *role_cmd* to NONE.

```
PROCEDURE DBMS_SESSION.SET_SQL_TRACE
    (sql_trace IN BOOLEAN);
```

Turns SQL tracing on or off in the session according to *sql_trace* (TRUE = on, FALSE = off).

```
FUNCTION DBMS_SESSION.UNIQUE_SESSION_ID
RETURN VARCHAR2;
```

Returns a string identifier unique to the session up to 24 bytes in length.

DBMS_SHARED_POOL

DBMS_SHARED_POOL contains programs to help manage the Oracle Shared Global Area (SGA) shared pool.

```
PROCEDURE DBMS_SHARED_POOL.ABORTED_REQUEST_THRESHOLD
    (threshold_size IN NUMBER);
```

Sets the maximum object size for which the shared pool will flush other objects to make room. Attempts to load objects larger than *threshold_size* bytes produce ORA-04031 errors if sufficient space is not available.

```
PROCEDURE DBMS_SHARED_POOL.KEEP
    (name IN VARCHAR2
    ,flag IN CHAR DEFAULT 'P');
```

Pins the object identified by *name* in the shared pool. The object's type is identified by *flag*: "P" or "p" for package, procedure, or function; "Q" or "q" for sequences; and "R" or "r" for triggers. Specifies any other character *flag* to pin a cursor identified by address and hash value (from V$SQLAREA) in *name*.

```
PROCEDURE DBMS_SHARED_POOL.SIZES
    (minsize IN NUMBER);
```

Displays objects and cursors in the shared pool that exceed *minsize* kilobytes in size.

```
PROCEDURE DBMS_SHARED_POOL.UNKEEP
    (name IN VARCHAR2
    ,flag IN CHAR DEFAULT 'P');
```

Unpins the object of type *flag* and identified by *name* from the shared pool. Valid *flag* values are the same values as for DBMS_SHARED_POOL.KEEP.

DBMS_SPACE

DBMS_SPACE contains procedures that provide internal space utilization and freelist information about table, index, and cluster segments.

```
PROCEDURE DBMS_SPACE.FREE_BLOCKS
    (segment_owner IN VARCHAR2
    ,segment_name IN VARCHAR2
    ,segment_type IN VARCHAR2
    ,freelist_group_id IN NUMBER
    ,free_blks OUT NUMBER
    ,scan_limit IN NUMBER DEFAULT NULL
  [ ,partition_name IN VARCHAR2 DEFAULT NULL ]);
```

Returns into *free_blks* the number of blocks on the freelist for segment *segment_name* of type *segment_type* (TABLE, INDEX, or CLUSTER) owned by *segment_owner* in partition *partition_name* (optional, and Oracle8 only). *Scan_limit* (optional) limits the number of free blocks scanned.

```
PROCEDURE DBMS_SPACE.UNUSED_SPACE
    (segment_owner IN VARCHAR2
    ,segment_name IN VARCHAR2
    ,segment_type IN VARCHAR2
    ,total_blocks OUT NUMBER
    ,total_bytes OUT NUMBER
    ,unused_blocks OUT NUMBER
    ,unused_bytes OUT NUMBER
    ,last_used_extent_file_id OUT NUMBER
    ,last_used_extent_block_id OUT NUMBER
    ,last_used_block OUT NUMBER
  [ ,partition_name IN VARCHAR2 DEFAULT NULL ]);
```

Returns the highwater mark (*last_used_extent_file_id*, *last_used_extent_block_id*, and *last_used_block*), space used (*total_blocks*, *total_bytes*), and space unused (*unused_blocks*, *unused_bytes*) in segment *segment_name* of type *segment_type* (TABLE, INDEX, or CLUSTER) owned by

segment_owner in partition *partition_name*. Optional, and
Oracle8 only.

DBMS_SQL

DBMS_SQL provides routines for using dynamic SQL within
PL/SQL. For Oracle8, this is the routine that provides support
for array operations in PL/SQL.

```
PROCEDURE DBMS_SQL.BIND_ARRAY
    (c IN INTEGER
    ,name IN VARCHAR2
    ,<table_variable IN datatype>
    [,index1 IN INTEGER
     ,index2 IN INTEGER]);
```

Binds the *table_variable* array to the placeholder *name* in
the parsed (but not executed) SQL statement in the cursor
c (returned by the OPEN_CURSOR call). For Oracle8, used
to perform array processing. The *<table_variable IN
datatype>* can be any of the following:

```
n_tab IN DBMS_SQL.NUMBER_TABLE
c_tab IN DBMS_SQL.VARCHAR2_TABLE
d_tab IN DBMS_SQL.DATE_TABLE
bl_tab IN DBMS_SQL.BLOB_TABLE
cl_tab IN DBMS_SQL.CLOB_TABLE
bf_tab IN DBMS_SQL.BFILE_TABLE
```

The optional argument *index1* defines the lower bound
(first row) within the table and *index2* defines the upper
bound (last row). Oracle 8 only.

```
PROCEDURE DBMS_SQL.BIND_VARIABLE
    (c IN INTEGER
    ,name IN VARCHAR2
    ,value IN NUMBER | VARACHAR2 | DATE | BLOB | CLOB
        CHARACTER SET ANY_CS | BFILE
    [,out_value_size IN INTEGER]);
```

Binds the scalar *value* to the placeholder *name* in the
parsed SQL statement in the cursor *c*, optionally with
maximum expected size of *value* being *out_value_size*.

```
PROCEDURE DBMS_SQL.BIND_VARIABLE_CHAR
    (c IN INTEGER
    ,name IN VARCHAR2
```

```
        ,value IN CHAR CHARACTER SET ANY_CS
   [,out_value_size IN INTEGER]);
```

Binds the scalar CHAR/NCHAR *value* to the placeholder
name in the parsed SQL statement in the cursor *c*, optionally with maximum expected size of *value* being *out_
value_size*.

```
PROCEDURE DBMS_SQL.BIND_VARIABLE_RAW
    (c IN INTEGER
    ,name IN VARCHAR2
    ,value IN RAW
   [,out_value_size IN INTEGER]);
```

Binds the scalar RAW *value* to the placeholder *name* in
the parsed SQL statement in the cursor *c* (returned by the
OPEN_CURSOR call), optionally with maximum expected
size of *value* being *out_value_size*.

```
PROCEDURE DBMS_SQL.BIND_VARIABLE_ROWID
    (c IN INTEGER
    ,name IN VARCHAR2
    ,value IN ROWID);
```

Binds the scalar ROWID *value* to the placeholder *name* in
the parsed SQL statement in the cursor *c*.

```
PROCEDURE DBMS_SQL.CLOSE_CURSOR
    (c IN OUT INTEGER);
```

Closes cursor *c*.

```
PROCEDURE DBMS_SQL.COLUMN_VALUE
    (c IN INTEGER
    ,position IN INTEGER
    ,value OUT NUMBER | VARCHAR | DATE | BLOB | CLOB
        CHARACTER SET ANY_CS | BFILE | MLSLABEL );
   [,column_error OUT NUMBER
   [,actual_length OUT INTEGER]]);
```

Transfers the contents of column number *position* in the
SELECT list of the fetched cursor *c* into the variable *value*,
optionally setting *actual_length* to the pre-truncated length
in bytes, and *column_error* to the error code for the specified value. Truncation may occur due to a difference in
size between the retrieved value in the cursor and the variable length. MLSLABEL is for Trusted Oracle only.

```
PROCEDURE DBMS_SQL.COLUMN_VALUE
    (c IN INTEGER
    ,position IN INTEGER
    ,<table_parameter IN table_type>);
```

Transfers the array contents of column number *position* in
the SELECT list of the fetched array from cursor *c* into the
PL/SQL table. For Oracle8 only, the *table_parameter* and
table_type can be any of the following:

```
n_tab IN DBMS_SQL.NUMBER_TABLE
c_tab IN DBMS_SQL.VARCHAR2_TABLE
d_tab IN DBMS_SQL.DATE_TABLE
bl_tab IN DBMS_SQL.BLOB_TABLE
cl_tab IN DBMS_SQL.CLOB_TABLE
bf_tab IN DBMS_SQL.BFILE_TABLE
```

```
PROCEDURE DBMS_SQL.COLUMN_VALUE_CHAR
    (c IN INTEGER
    ,position IN INTEGER
    ,value OUT CHAR CHARACTER SET ANY_CS
    [,column_error OUT NUMBER
    [,actual_length OUT INTEGER]]);
```

Transfers the contents of column number *position* in the
SELECT list of the fetched cursor *c* into the CHAR/NCHAR
variable *value*, optionally setting *actual_length* to the pre-
truncated length in characters, and the *column_error* to the
error code for the specified value. Truncation may occur
due to a difference in size between the retrieved value in
the cursor and the variable length.

```
PROCEDURE DBMS_SQL.COLUMN_VALUE_LONG
    (c IN INTEGER
    ,position IN INTEGER
    ,length IN INTEGER
    ,offset IN INTEGER
    ,value OUT VARCHAR2
    ,value_length OUT INTEGER);
```

Transfers the contents of column number *position* in the
SELECT list of the fetched cursor *c* into the VARCHAR2
variable *value*, starting *offset* bytes into the LONG column
and extending for *length* bytes. Also sets *value_length* to
the actual length of the retrieved value.

```
PROCEDURE DBMS_SQL.COLUMN_VALUE_RAW
    (c IN INTEGER
    ,position IN INTEGER
    ,value OUT RAW
[,column_error OUT NUMBER
[,actual_length OUT INTEGER]]);
```

Transfers the contents of column number *position* in the
SELECT list of the fetched cursor *c* into the RAW variable
value, optionally setting *actual_length* to the pre-truncated length in bytes, and the *column_error* to the error
code for the specified value. Truncation may occur due to
a difference in size between the retrieved value in the
cursor and the variable length.

```
PROCEDURE DBMS_SQL.COLUMN_VALUE_ROWID
    (c IN INTEGER
    ,position IN INTEGER
    ,value OUT ROWID);
[,column_error OUT NUMBER
[,actual_length OUT INTEGER]]);
```

Transfers the contents of column number *position* in the
SELECT list of the fetched cursor *c* into the ROWID variable *value*, optionally setting *actual_length* to the pre-
truncated length in bytes, and the *column_error* to the
error code for the specified value. Truncation may occur
due to a difference in size between the retrieved value in
the cursor and the variable length.

```
PROCEDURE DBMS_SQL.DEFINE_ARRAY
    (c IN INTEGER
    ,position IN INTEGER
    ,<table_parameter IN table_type>
    ,cnt IN INTEGER
    ,lower_bound IN INTEGER);
```

Defines the datatype and size of the elements in the fetch
array for column number *position* in the SELECT list of the
cursor *c* as the same datatype and size as the nested table
table_parameter, beginning with row *lower_bound*, and
having a maximum array size of *cnt* rows. For Oracle8,
table_parameter and *table_type* can be any of these:

```
n_tab IN DBMS_SQL.NUMBER_TABLE
c_tab IN DBMS_SQL.VARCHAR2_TABLE
```

```
          d_tab IN DBMS_SQL.DATE_TABLE
          bl_tab IN DBMS_SQL.BLOB_TABLE
          cl_tab IN DBMS_SQL.CLOB_TABLE
          bf_tab IN DBMS_SQL.BFILE_TABLE

PROCEDURE DBMS_SQL.DEFINE_COLUMN
     (c IN INTEGER
     ,position IN INTEGER
     ,column IN NUMBER | DATE | BLOB | CLOB CHARACTER SET
         ANY_CD | BFILE | MLSLABEL);
```

The variable or expression *column* defines the datatype for column number *position* in the SELECT list of the cursor *c*. MLSLABEL is for Trusted Oracle only.

```
PROCEDURE DBMS_SQL.DEFINE_COLUMN
     (c IN INTEGER
     ,position IN INTEGER
     ,column IN VARCHAR2 CHARACTER SET ANY_CS
     ,column_size IN INTEGER);
```

The variable or expression *column* defines the datatype as VARCHAR2/NVARCHAR2 and size as *column_size* characters for column number *position* in the SELECT list of the cursor *c*.

```
PROCEDURE DBMS_SQL.DEFINE_COLUMN_CHAR
     (c IN INTEGER
     ,position IN INTEGER
     ,column IN CHAR CHARACTER SET ANY_CS
     ,column_size IN INTEGER);
```

The variable or expression *column* defines the datatype as CHAR/NCHAR and size as *column_size* characters for column number *position* in the SELECT list of the cursor *c*.

```
PROCEDURE DBMS_SQL.DEFINE_COLUMN_LONG
     (c IN INTEGER
     ,position IN INTEGER);
```

Defines the datatype as LONG for column number *position* in the SELECT list of the cursor *c*.

```
PROCEDURE DBMS_SQL.DEFINE_COLUMN_RAW
     (c IN INTEGER
     ,position IN INTEGER
     ,column IN RAW
     ,column_size IN INTEGER);
```

The variable or expression *column* defines the datatype
as RAW of size *column_size* bytes for column number
position in the SELECT list of the cursor *c*.

```
PROCEDURE DBMS_SQL.DEFINE_COLUMN_ROWID
    (c IN INTEGER
    ,position IN INTEGER
    ,column IN ROWID);
```

The variable or expression *column* defines the datatype as
ROWID for column number *position* in the SELECT list of
the cursor *c*.

```
PROCEDURE DBMS_SQL.DESCRIBE_COLUMNS
    (c IN INTEGER
    ,col_cnt OUT INTEGER
    ,desc_t OUT DESC_TAB);
```

Populates PL/SQL table *desc_t* of type DBMS_SQL.DESC_
REC with the description of columns of cursor *c*. *col_cnt* is
the number of columns in *c* and the number of rows in
desc_t.

```
FUNCTION DBMS_SQL.EXECUTE
    (c IN INTEGER)
RETURN INTEGER;
```

For INSERT, UPDATE, or DELETE statements, returns the
number of rows processed by executing the cursor *c*. For
all other SQL statements, executes the cursor *c* and returns
an undefined value.

```
FUNCTION DBMS_SQL.EXECUTE_AND_FETCH
    (c IN INTEGER
    ,exact IN BOOLEAN DEFAULT FALSE)
RETURN INTEGER;
```

Returns the number of rows fetched by executing and
fetching cursor *c*. Raises an exception if more than one
row is fetched when *exact* is set to TRUE. Multiple rows
require Oracle8 and array processing.

```
FUNCTION DBMS_SQL.FETCH_ROWS
    (c IN INTEGER)
RETURN INTEGER;
```

Fetches and returns the number of rows fetched from
cursor *c*, or 0 (zero) when there are no more rows to fetch.

```
FUNCTION DBMS_SQL.IS_OPEN
    (c IN INTEGER)
RETURN BOOLEAN;
```

Returns TRUE if cursor *c* is open, FALSE otherwise.

```
FUNCTION DBMS_SQL.LAST_ERROR_POSITION
RETURN INTEGER;
```

Returns the byte offset in the SQL statement where the last error occurred. Must be called immediately after an EXECUTE or EXECUTE_AND_FETCH (typically in the exception handler).

```
FUNCTION DBMS_SQL.LAST_ROW_COUNT
RETURN INTEGER;
```

Returns the total number of rows fetched so far—similar to the %ROWCOUNT attribute of static cursors.

```
FUNCTION DBMS_SQL.LAST_ROW_ID
RETURN ROWID;
```

Returns the ROWID of the most recently fetched row. Must be called immediately after a FETCH_ROWS or EXECUTE_AND_FETCH.

```
FUNCTION DBMS_SQL.LAST_SQL_FUNCTION_CODE
RETURN INTEGER;
```

Returns the SQL function code for the SQL statement. A complete list of these function codes can be found in the Oracle Corporation's Server Reference Manual in the section describing the table column V$SESSION.COMMAND.

```
FUNCTION DBMS_SQL.OPEN_CURSOR
RETURN INTEGER;
```

Returns an INTEGER pointer to memory allocated for a dynamic cursor.

```
PROCEDURE DBMS_SQL.PARSE
    (c IN INTEGER
    ,statement IN VARCHAR2
    ,language_flag IN INTEGER);
```

Parses a SQL *statement* less than 32K bytes in length and associates it with cursor *c*, following database behavior specified by *language_flag* (either DBMS_SQL.NATIVE, DBMS_SQL.V7, or DBMS_SQL.V6). Do not terminate your

SQL string with a semicolon unless it is a PL/SQL block.
For DDL statements (e.g., TRUNCATE TABLE), this also
executes the statement.

```
PROCEDURE DBMS_SQL.PARSE
    (c IN INTEGER
    ,statement IN VARCHAR2S
    ,lb IN INTEGER
    ,ub IN INTEGER
    ,lfflg IN BOOLEAN
    ,language_flag IN INTEGER);
```

Parses a SQL *statement* contained in rows *lb* through *ub* in
the PL/SQL table and associates it with cursor *c*, following
database behavior specified by *language_flag* (either
DBMS_SQL.NATIVE, DBMS_SQL.V7, or DBMS_SQL.V6),
and appending a line feed after each row from *statement* if
lfflg is set to TRUE.

```
PROCEDURE DBMS_SQL.VARIABLE_VALUE
    (c IN INTEGER
    ,name IN VARCHAR2
    ,value OUT NUMBER | VARCHAR2 | DATE | BLOB | CLOB
        CHARACTER SET ANY_CS| BFILE | MLSLABEL);
```

Retrieves the value of the host variable *name* in cursor *c*
into the PL/SQL NUMBER variable *value*. MLSLABEL is for
Trusted Oracle only.

```
PROCEDURE DBMS_SQL.VARIABLE_VALUE
    (c IN INTEGER
    ,name IN VARCHAR2
    ,value IN <table_type>);
```

Retrieves the values of the host variable *name* in cursor *c*
into the PL/SQL table *value*. For Oracle8 only, the *table_
type* can be one of the following:

```
DBMS_SQL.NUMBER_TABLE
DBMS_SQL.VARCHAR2_TABLE
DBMS_SQL.DATE_TABLE
DBMS_SQL.BLOB_TABLE
DBMS_SQL.CLOB_TABLE
DBMS_SQL.BFILE_TABLE
```

```
PROCEDURE DBMS_SQL.VARIABLE_VALUE_CHAR
    (c IN INTEGER
    ,name IN VARCHAR2
    ,value OUT CHAR CHARACTER SET ANY_CS);
```

Retrieves the value of the host variable *name* in cursor *c*
into the CHAR/NCHAR table *value*.

```
PROCEDURE DBMS_SQL.VARIABLE_VALUE_RAW
    (c IN INTEGER
    ,name IN VARCHAR2
    ,value OUT RAW);
```

Retrieves the value of the host variable *name* in cursor *c*
into the RAW variable *value*.

```
PROCEDURE DBMS_SQL.VARIABLE_VALUE_ROWID
    (c IN INTEGER
    ,name IN VARCHAR2
    ,value OUT ROWID);
```

Retrieves the value of the host variable *name* in cursor *c*
into the ROWID variable *value*.

DBMS_STANDARD

DBMS_STANDARD contains "kernel extensions to package
STANDARD." These include functions and procedures for use
in triggers to support transactions. These functions and procedures, like those in package STANDARD, are special in that
they do not need to be qualified with the owner or package
name, and are usually assumed to be part of the
PL/SQL language.

```
PROCEDURE DBMS_STANDARD.RAISE_APPLICATION_ERROR
    (num BINARY_INTEGER
    ,msg VARCHAR2
    ,keeperrorstack boolean default FALSE);
```

Raises PL/SQL exception *num*, together with text *msg* from
a stored program. The error can be placed together with
any other errors on the error stack. If *keeperrorstack* is set
to TRUE, default behavior is to replace the error stack with
this single exception. *num* can range from –20999 to
–20000, and *msg* can be up to 2048 bytes long.

```
FUNCTION INSERTING RETURN boolean;
FUNCTION DELETING  RETURN boolean;
FUNCTION UPDATING  RETURN boolean;
FUNCTION UPDATING (colnam VARCHAR2) RETURN boolean;
```

Conditional predicates used to determine the type of Data
Manipulation Language (DML) operation that caused a
trigger to fire. These functions are only useful within triggers; for example "...IF INSERTING THEN...."

```
PROCEDURE COMMIT;
PROCEDURE COMMIT_CM (vc VARCHAR2);
PROCEDURE ROLLBACK_NR;
PROCEDURE ROLLBACK_SV(save_point VARCHAR2);
PROCEDURE SAVEPOINT(save_point VARCHAR2);
PROCEDURE SET_TRANSACTION_USE(vc VARCHAR2);
```

These procedures support transaction control. They are
analogous to the SQL statements: COMMIT, COMMIT
COMMENT, ROLLBACK, ROLLBACK TO SAVEPOINT,
SAVEPOINT, and SET TRANSACTION USE ROLLBACK
SEGMENT.

DBMS_SYSTEM

DBMS_SYSTEM contains procedures for setting special
internal trace events, including SQL tracing, at the session
level.

```
PROCEDURE DBMS_SYSTEM.READ_EV
    (iev BINARY_INTEGER
    ,oev OUT BINARY_INTEGER);
```

Returns the current session's event level setting for trace
event number *iev* into variable *oev*.

```
PROCEDURE DBMS_SYSTEM.SET_EV
    (si BINARY_INTEGER
    ,se BINARY_INTEGER
    ,ev BINARY_INTEGER
    ,le BINARY_INTEGER
    ,nm IN VARCHAR2);
```

Sets the level for event number *ev* in the session identified
by sid *si* and serial number *se* to the value specified by *le*.
Variable *nm* is used to specify the event name.

```
PROCEDURE DBMS_SYSTEM.SET_SQL_TRACE_IN_SESSION
    (sid IN NUMBER
    ,serial# IN NUMBER
    ,sql_trace IN BOOLEAN);
```

Turns SQL tracing on or off in the session identified by sid (*sid*) and serial number (*serial#*) according to the value of *sql_trace* (TRUE = on; FALSE = off).

DBMS_TRANSACTION

DBMS_TRANSACTION contains a number of programs for local and distributed transaction management.

```
PROCEDURE DBMS_TRANSACTION.ADVISE_COMMIT;
```

Advises remote databases that in-doubt distributed transactions should be committed if possible.

```
PROCEDURE DBMS_TRANSACTION.ADVISE_NOTHING;
```

Removes advice from remote databases regarding in-doubt distributed transactions.

```
PROCEDURE DBMS_TRANSACTION.ADVISE_ROLLBACK;
```

Advises remote databases that in-doubt distributed transactions should be rolled back.

```
PROCEDURE DBMS_TRANSACTION.BEGIN_DISCRETE_TRANSACTION;
```

Sets the current transaction to use discrete transaction processing.

```
PROCEDURE DBMS_TRANSACTION.COMMIT;
```

Commits the current transaction.

```
PROCEDURE DBMS_TRANSACTION.COMMIT_COMMENT
    (cmnt IN VARCHAR2);
```

Commits the current transaction and sends *cmnt* as the in-doubt transaction comment to remote databases during distributed transactions.

```
PROCEDURE DBMS_TRANSACTION.COMMIT_FORCE
    (xid IN VARCHAR2
    [,scn IN VARCHAR2 DEFAULT NULL)];
```

Forces the local portion of the in-doubt distributed transaction identified by transaction id *xid* and (optionally) system change number *scn* to commit.

```
FUNCTION DBMS_TRANSACTION.LOCAL_TRANSACTION_ID
    (create_transaction IN BOOLEAN := FALSE)
RETURN VARCHAR2;
```

Returns Oracle's unique identifier for the current transaction, optionally beginning a new transaction when *create_transaction* is TRUE.

```
PROCEDURE DBMS_TRANSACTION.PURGE_LOST_DB_ENTRY
    (xid IN VARCHAR2);
```

Forces Oracle to purge all local entries for the distributed transaction identified by *xid* when a participating node has been permanently lost.

```
PROCEDURE DBMS_TRANSACTION.PURGE_MIXED
    (xid IN VARCHAR2);
```

Forces Oracle to purge local entries for the mixed outcome distributed transaction identified locally by *xid*.

```
PROCEDURE DBMS_TRANSACTION.READ_ONLY;
```

Establishes transaction-level read consistency, where all queries return read-consistent images of data as of the transaction's start time.

```
PROCEDURE DBMS_TRANSACTION.READ_WRITE;
```

Establishes statement-level read consistency, which is also the default behavior.

```
PROCEDURE DBMS_TRANSACTION.ROLLBACK;
```

Rolls back the current transaction.

```
PROCEDURE DBMS_TRANSACTION.ROLLBACK_FORCE
    (xid IN VARCHAR2);
```

Rolls back the local portion of the in-doubt distributed transaction identified by *xid*.

```
PROCEDURE DBMS_TRANSACTION.ROLLBACK_SAVEPOINT
    (savept IN VARCHAR2);
```

Rolls back the current transaction to the savepoint *savept*.

```
PROCEDURE DBMS_TRANSACTION.SAVEPOINT
    (savept IN VARCHAR2);
```

Sets a savepoint named *savept* in the current transaction.

```
FUNCTION DBMS_TRANSACTION.STEP_ID
RETURN NUMBER;
```

Returns a unique positive integer that orders the DML operations of the current transaction.

```
PROCEDURE DBMS_TRANSACTION.USE_ROLLBACK_SEGMENT
    (rb_name IN VARCHAR2);
```

Assigns the current transaction to rollback segment *rb_ name*.

DBMS_UTILITY

DBMS_UTILITY provides procedures and functions to perform a number of useful tasks, including parsing and tokenizing name references, obtaining database configuration information, analyzing objects, obtaining error and call stack information, and timing code execution.

```
PROCEDURE DBMS_UTILITY.ANALYZE_DATABASE
    (method IN VARCHAR2
    ,estimate_rows IN NUMBER DEFAULT NULL
    ,estimate_percent IN NUMBER DEFAULT NULL
    ,method_opt IN VARCHAR2 DEFAULT NULL);
```

Analyzes all tables, clusters, and indexes in the database using option *method* (ESTIMATE, NULL, or DELETE). When *method* is ESTIMATE, either *estimate_rows* or *estimate_percent* must be specified to identify sample size. Additional analyze options specifiable by *method_opt* are: FOR TABLE; FOR ALL COLUMNS [SIZE *N*]; FOR ALL INDEXED COLUMNS [SIZE *N*]; or FOR ALL INDEXES.

```
PROCEDURE DBMS_UTILITY.ANALYZE_PART_OBJECT
    (schema IN VARCHAR2 DEFAULT NULL
    ,object_name IN VARCHAR2 DEFAULT NULL
    ,object_type IN CHAR DEFAULT 'T'
    ,command_type IN CHAR DEFAULT 'E'
    ,command_opt IN VARCHAR2 DEFAULT NULL
    ,sample_clause IN VARCHAR2
        DEFAULT 'SAMPLE 5 PERCENT');
```

Analyzes the partitioned table or index *object_name* owned by *schema* of type *object_type* (T = TABLE, I = INDEX) in parallel using Oracle job queue processes. *command_type* indicates the type of analysis to perform

---

and *command_opt* specifies additional options. *sample_clause* specifies sample size when *command_type* is E (estimate) using 'SAMPLE N ROWS' or 'SAMPLE N PERCENT'. Oracle8 only.

Valid *command_type* values are: C for compute statistics, E for estimate statistics, D for delete statistics, or V for validate structure.

Valid *command_opt* values for *command_type* C or T are: FOR TABLE, FOR ALL LOCAL INDEXES, FOR ALL COLUMNS, or any combination of FOR options of the ANALYZE command.

Valid *command_opt* values for *command_type* V are: CASCADE when *object_type* is T (table).

```
PROCEDURE DBMS_UTILITY.ANALYZE_SCHEMA
    (schema IN VARCHAR2
    ,method IN VARCHAR2
    ,estimate_rows IN NUMBER DEFAULT NULL
    ,estimate_percent IN NUMBER DEFAULT NULL
    ,method_opt IN VARCHAR2 DEFAULT NULL);
```

Analyzes all tables, clusters, and indexes in *schema* using *method* (ESTIMATE, NULL, or DELETE). When *method* is ESTIMATE, either *estimate_rows* or *estimate_percent* must be specified to identify sample size. Additional analyze options specifiable by *method_opt* are: FOR TABLE, FOR ALL COLUMNS [SIZE *N*], FOR ALL INDEXED COLUMNS [SIZE *N*], or FOR ALL INDEXES.

```
PROCEDURE DBMS_UTILITY.COMMA_TO_TABLE
    (list IN VARCHAR2
    ,tablen OUT BINARY_INTEGER
    ,tab OUT UNCL_ARRAY);
```

Parses the comma-delimited *list* and returns the tokens in the PL/SQL table *tab* of type DBMS_UTILITY.UNCL_ARRAY. The number of rows in *tab* is returned in *tablen*.

```
PROCEDURE DBMS_UTILITY.COMPILE_SCHEMA
    (schema IN VARCHAR2);
```

Compiles all stored PL/SQL programs (procedures, functions, and packages) owned by *schema*.

```
FUNCTION DBMS_UTILITY.DATA_BLOCK_ADDRESS_BLOCK
    (dba IN NUMBER)
RETURN NUMBER;
```

Returns the block offset number of the data block address
specified in *dba*.

```
FUNCTION DBMS_UTILITY.DATA_BLOCK_ADDRESS_FILE
    (dba IN NUMBER)
RETURN NUMBER;
```

Returns the file number component of the data block
address specified in *dba*.

```
PROCEDURE DBMS_UTILITY.DB_VERSION
    (version OUT VARCHAR2
    ,compatibility OUT VARCHAR2);
```

Returns the Oracle version of the database in *version* and
the setting of the *INIT.ORA* COMPATIBLE parameter in
compatibility (or NULL). Oracle8 only.

```
PROCEDURE DBMS_UTILITY.EXEC_DDL_STATEMENT
    (parse_string IN VARCHAR2);
```

Executes the DDL statement specified by *parse_string*.
Oracle8 only.

```
FUNCTION DBMS_UTILITY.FORMAT_CALL_STACK
RETURN VARCHAR2;
```

Returns the current PL/SQL call stack as a formatted string.

```
FUNCTION DBMS_UTILITY.FORMAT_ERROR_STACK
RETURN VARCHAR2;
```

Returns the current PL/SQL error stack as a formatted
string.

```
FUNCTION DBMS_UTILITY.GET_HASH_VALUE
    (name IN VARCHAR2
    ,base IN NUMBER
    ,hash_size IN NUMBER)
RETURN NUMBER;
```

Returns a hash function value for *name* with a minimum
possible value of *base* using a hash table of size *hash_size*.

```
FUNCTION DBMS_UTILITY.GET_PARAMETER_VALUE
    (parnam IN VARCHAR2
    ,intval IN OUT BINARY_INTEGER
```

```
    ,strval IN OUT VARCHAR2)
RETURN BINARY_INTEGER;
```

Returns information about the current setting of the database initialization (*INIT.ORA*) parameter *parnam*. Oracle8 only.

intval returns the following values:

- The value of a numeric *parnam*

- The length of a string *parnam*

- 0 for FALSE and 1 for TRUE when *parnam* is Boolean

strval returns NULL, or the value of a string parameter: 0 if the parameter is Boolean or numeric; 1 if the parameter is a string.

```
FUNCTION DBMS_UTILITY.GET_TIME
RETURN NUMBER;
```

Returns a number indicating the number of 1/100ths of a seconds elapsed since an (unknown) arbitrary time in the past.

```
FUNCTION DBMS_UTILITY.IS_PARALLEL_SERVER
RETURN BOOLEAN;
```

Returns TRUE if the instance is running in parallel server mode, and FALSE otherwise.

```
FUNCTION DBMS_UTILITY.MAKE_DATA_BLOCK_ADDRESS
    (file IN NUMBER
    ,block IN NUMBER)
RETURN NUMBER;
```

Returns a valid data block address for *file* at block offset *block*.

```
PROCEDURE DBMS_UTILITY.NAME_RESOLVE
    (name IN VARCHAR2
    ,context IN NUMBER
    ,schema OUT VARCHAR2
    ,part1 OUT VARCHAR2
    ,part2 OUT VARCHAR2
    ,dblink OUT VARCHAR2
    ,part1_type OUT NUMBER
    ,object_number OUT NUMBER);
```

Resolves the reference *name* and returns specific identification information about the object referenced as follows: *schema* is the object's owner; *part1* is the object name or package name for a package; *part2* is the program name when object is a package; *dblink* is the database link if *name* resolves to a remote object; *part1_type* identifies the type of object; *object_number* is the local object number or NULL if *name* could not be fully resolved locally.

part1_type is 5 if the object is a synonym; 7 if the object is a procedure; 8 if the object is a function; 9 if the object is a package.

Note that *context* must be set to 1.

```
PROCEDURE DBMS_UTILITY.NAME_TOKENIZE
    (name IN VARCHAR2
    ,a OUT VARCHAR2
    ,b OUT VARCHAR2
    ,c OUT VARCHAR2
    ,dblink OUT VARCHAR2
    ,nextpos OUT BINARY_INTEGER);
```

Uses the PL/SQL parser to tokenize the reference *name* into its constituent components according to the following format:

a [. *b* [. *c*]] [*@dblink*]

nextpos is the starting position of the next token.

```
FUNCTION DBMS_UTILITY.PORT_STRING
RETURN VARCHAR2;
```

Returns a string with operating system-specific identifying information about the version of Oracle that is running.

```
PROCEDURE DBMS_UTILITY.TABLE_TO_COMMA
    (tab IN UNCL_ARRAY
    ,tablen OUT BINARY_INTEGER
    ,list OUT VARCHAR2);
```

Converts the PL/SQL table *tab* of type DBMS_UTILITY.UNCL_ARRAY into a comma-delimited string returned in *list*, with the number of rows converted returned in *tablen*.

UTL_FILE

UTL_FILE allows PL/SQL programs to read from and write to operating system files on the server where the Oracle database resides.

```
PROCEDURE UTL_FILE.FCLOSE
    (file IN OUT FILE_TYPE);
```

Closes the file identified by file handle *file* and sets the value of file id to NULL.

```
PROCEDURE UTL_FILE.FCLOSE_ALL;
```

Closes all opened files; however, the id fields of any file handles will not be set to NULL.

```
PROCEDURE UTL_FILE.FFLUSH
    (file IN FILE_TYPE);
```

Forces any buffered data for file handle *file* to be written out immediately.

```
FUNCTION UTL_FILE.FOPEN
    (location IN VARCHAR2
    ,filename IN VARCHAR2
    ,open_mode IN VARCHAR2)
RETURN FILE_TYPE;
```

Returns a file handle of type UTL_FILE.FILE_TYPE upon successfully opening file *filename* in directory *location* in mode *open_mode*, or raises an exception.

Valid *open_mode* values are:

R = open file in read-only mode.
W = open file in read-write mode and replace contents.
A = open file in read-write mode and append to contents.

Valid *location* values are directories specified by the Oracle initialization parameter UTL_FILE_DIR.

```
PROCEDURE UTL_FILE.GET_LINE
    (file IN FILE_TYPE
    ,buffer OUT VARCHAR2);
```

Reads the next line in file handle *file* into *buffer*. Raises NO_DATA_FOUND exception when reading past end of file and VALUE_ERROR exception when *buffer* is too small for the data.

```
FUNCTION UTL_FILE.IS_OPEN
   (file IN FILE_TYPE)
RETURN BOOLEAN;
```

Returns TRUE if the file handle *file* is currently open in any mode and FALSE otherwise.

```
PROCEDURE UTL_FILE.NEW_LINE
   (file IN FILE_TYPE
   ,lines IN NATURAL := 1);
```

Places *lines* newline characters into file handle *file*.

```
PROCEDURE UTL_FILE.PUT
   (file IN FILE_TYPE
   ,buffer IN VARCHAR2);
```

Places the data in *buffer* into file handle *file* without a newline terminator.

```
PROCEDURE UTL_FILE.PUT_LINE
   (file IN FILE_TYPE
   ,buffer IN VARCHAR2);
```

Places the data in *buffer* into file handle *file* with a newline character appended.

```
PROCEDURE UTL_FILE.PUTF
   (file IN FILE_TYPE
   ,format IN VARCHAR2
   ,arg1 IN VARCHAR2 DEFAULT NULL
   ,arg2 IN VARCHAR2 DEFAULT NULL
   ,arg3 IN VARCHAR2 DEFAULT NULL
   ,arg4 IN VARCHAR2 DEFAULT NULL
   ,arg5 IN VARCHAR2 DEFAULT NULL);
```

Writes a formatted message out to file handle *file* using *format* as the template, replacing up to five %s format elements with the values of *arg1–arg5*. *format* can contain the following items: any literal text; %s indicating *argN* substitution (up to five allowed); or %n indicating newline (any number allowed).

UTL_RAW

UTL_RAW provides routines for accessing and manipulating RAW datatypes. These routines perform conversions, divisions, combinations, and bitwise operations on RAW datatypes.

```
FUNCTION UTL_RAW.BIT_AND
    (r1 IN RAW
    ,r2 IN RAW)
RETURN RAW;
```

Returns the bitwise logical AND of *r1* and *r2*.

```
FUNCTION UTL_RAW.BIT_COMPLEMENT
    (r1 IN RAW
    ,r2 IN RAW)
RETURN RAW;
```

Returns the bitwise logical complement of *r1* and *r2*.

```
FUNCTION UTL_RAW.BIT_OR
    (r1 IN RAW
    ,r2 IN RAW)
RETURN RAW;
```

Returns the bitwise logical OR of *r1* and *r2*.

```
FUNCTION UTL_RAW.BIT_XOR
    (r1 IN RAW
    ,r2 IN RAW)
RETURN RAW;
```

Returns the bitwise logical XOR of *r1* and *r2*.

```
FUNCTION UTL_RAW.CAST_TO_RAW
    (c IN VARCHAR2)
RETURN RAW;
```

Returns VARCHAR2 *c* to RAW, converting datatype only.

```
FUNCTION UTL_RAW.CAST_TO_VARCHAR2
    (r IN RAW)
RETURN VARCHAR2;
```

Returns RAW *c* to VARCHAR2, converting datatype only.

```
FUNCTION UTL_RAW.COMPARE
    (r1 IN RAW
    ,r2 IN RAW
    ,pad IN RAW DEFAULT NULL)
RETURN NUMBER;
```

Returns 0 if *r1* and *r2* are identical. Returns first byte position of difference in *r1* and *r2*. If *r1* and *r2* are different lengths, right pad the shorter with *pad*.

```
FUNCTION UTL_RAW.CONCAT
    (r1 IN RAW DEFAULT NULL
    ,r2 IN RAW DEFAULT NULL
```

```
    ,r3 IN RAW DEFAULT NULL
    ,r4 IN RAW DEFAULT NULL
    ,r5 IN RAW DEFAULT NULL
    ,r6 IN RAW DEFAULT NULL
    ,r7 IN RAW DEFAULT NULL
    ,r8 IN RAW DEFAULT NULL
    ,r9 IN RAW DEFAULT NULL
    ,r10 IN RAW DEFAULT NULL
    ,r11 IN RAW DEFAULT NULL
    ,r12 IN RAW DEFAULT NULL)
RETURN RAW;
```

Returns the concatenation of *r1* through *r12*. The result must be less than 32K. *r3* through *r12* are optional.

```
FUNCTION UTL_RAW.CONVERT
    (r IN RAW
    ,to_charset IN VARCHAR2
    ,from_charset IN VARCHAR2)
RETURN RAW;
```

Returns *r* in *to_charset* after conversion from *from_charset*. *from_charset* and *to_charset* are NLS character sets.

```
FUNCTION UTL_RAW.COPIES
    (r IN RAW
    ,n IN NUMBER)
RETURN RAW;
```

Concatenates *r*, *n* number of times, and returns the result.

```
FUNCTION UTL_RAW.LENGTH
    (r IN RAW)
RETURN NUMBER;
```

Returns the number of bytes in *r*.

```
FUNCTION UTL_RAW.OVERLAY
    (overlay_str IN RAW
    ,target IN RAW
    ,pos IN BINARY_INTEGER DEFAULT 1
    ,len IN BINARY_INTEGER DEFAULT NULL
    ,pad IN RAW DEFAULT NULL)
RETURN RAW;
```

Returns the *target* overlaid with the *overlay_str* string beginning *pos* bytes into *target* and continuing for *len* bytes, right padding with *pad* as necessary. If *pos* is greater than the length of *target,* fills the missing section with *pad.*

```
FUNCTION UTL_RAW.REVERSE
    (r IN RAW)
RETURN RAW;
```

Returns the bytes in *r* in reverse order.

```
FUNCTION UTL_RAW.SUBSTR
    (r IN RAW
    ,pos IN BINARY_INTEGER
    ,len IN BINARY_INTEGER DEFAULT NULL)
RETURN RAW;
```

Returns a portion of *r* beginning at *pos* and extending for *len* bytes.

```
FUNCTION UTL_RAW.TRANSLATE
    (r IN RAW
    ,from_set IN RAW
    ,to_set IN RAW)
RETURN RAW;
```

Returns the contents of *r,* translating bytes found in *from_set* to *to_set*. If *from_set* is longer than *to_set*, the unmatched bytes are removed from *r*.

```
FUNCTION UTL_RAW.TRANSLITERATE
    (r IN RAW
    ,to_set IN RAW DEFAULT NULL
    ,from_set IN RAW DEFAULT NULL
    ,pad IN RAW DEFAULT NULL)
RETURN RAW;
```

Returns the contents of *r,* translating bytes found in *from_set* to *to_set*. If *from_set* is longer than *to_set*, the unmatched bytes are translated to *pad*.

```
FUNCTION UTL_RAW.XRANGE
    (start_byte IN RAW DEFAULT NULL
    ,end_byte IN RAW DEFAULT NULL)
RETURN RAW;
```

Returns a raw string containing all bytes in order between *start_byte* and *end_byte*, inclusive. If *start_byte* is greater than *end_byte*, the result wraps from 0xFF to 0x00.

UTL_REF

UTL_REF contains routines for selecting and modifying instances of an object type in an object table. The name of the table does not have to be known. Oracle8.1 only.

```
PROCEDURE UTL_REF.DELETE_OBJECT
    (reference IN REF ANY);
```

Deletes the object (actually the row containing the object) identified by *reference*.

```
PROCEDURE UTL_REF.LOCK_OBJECT
    (reference IN REF ANY);
```

Locks the object referenced by *reference*.

```
PROCEDURE UTL_REF.LOCK_OBJECT
    (reference IN REF ANY
    ,object IN OUT ANY);
```

Locks the object referenced by *reference* and retrieves the object into *object*. Similar to a SELECT FOR UPDATE statement.

```
PROCEDURE UTL_REF.SELECT_OBJECT
    (reference IN REF ANY
    ,object IN OUT ANY);
```

Retrieves the object referenced by *reference* into *object*.

```
PROCEDURE UTL_REF.UPDATE_OBJECT
    (reference IN REF ANY
    ,object IN OUT ANY);
```

Replaces an object in the database identified by *reference* with the object *object*.

Built-in Functions

Built-in functions, implemented by Oracle in the STANDARD built-in package, are predefined functions that give you convenient ways to manipulate your data. There are six basic types of built-in functions, each described here in its own section:

- *Character functions* analyze and modify the contents of CHAR and VARCHAR2 string variables.

- *Numeric functions* are a full range of operations that manipulate numbers, including trigonometric, logarithmic, and exponential functions.

- *Date functions* are utilities that allow programmers to perform high-level actions on date variables, including date arithmetic.

- *Conversion functions* convert from one datatype to another, often formatting the output data at the same time.

- *LOB functions* allow operations on LOB (large object) data.

- *Miscellaneous functions* perform operations that don't fall into any of the other categories.

STANDARD contains definitions and functions for the PL/SQL language. These definitions include all of the PL/SQL datatypes, the named exceptions, and the functions and operators (which are defined as functions). Note that almost all STANDARD functions have corresponding SQL native functions.

Character Functions

Character functions parse names, concatenate strings, and perform other character operations.

```
FUNCTION ASCII
    (ch IN VARCHAR2 CHARACTER SET ANY_CS)
RETURN BINARY_INTEGER;
```

Returns the numeric ASCII code for *ch*.

```
FUNCTION CHR (n BINARY_INTEGER) RETURN VARCHAR2;
```

Returns the character associated with the numeric collating sequence *n*, according to the database's character set.

```
FUNCTION CONCAT
    (left IN VARCHAR2 CHARACTER SET ANY_CS
    ,right IN VARCHAR2 CHARACTER SET left%CHARSET)
RETURN VARCHAR2;
```

Returns the string *right* appended to string *left*.

```
FUNCTION INITCAP
    (ch IN VARCHAR2 CHARACTER SET ANY_CS)
RETURN VARCHAR2;
```

Returns the string *ch* with the first letter of each word in uppercase and all other letters in lowercase.

```
FUNCTION INSTR
    (str1 IN VARCHAR2 CHARACTER SET ANY_CS
    ,str2 IN VARCHAR2 CHARACTER SET str1%CHARSET
```

```
    ,pos BINARY_INTEGER := 1
    ,nth IN POSITIVE := 1)
RETURN BINARY_INTEGER;
```

Returns the character position of the *nth* appearance of
str2 in the string *str1*. The search begins *pos* characters into
str1 and continues for the length of *str1*. A negative *pos*
forces a right to left (backwards) search.

```
FUNCTION INSTRB
    (str1 IN VARCHAR2 CHARACTER SET ANY_CS
    ,str2 IN VARCHAR2 CHARACTER SET str1%CHARSET
    ,pos BINARY_INTEGER := 1
    ,nth IN POSITIVE := 1)
RETURN BINARY_INTEGER;
```

Same as INSTR except *pos* and *len* are expressed in bytes
(for multi-byte character sets).

```
FUNCTION LENGTH
    (ch IN VARCHAR2 CHARACTER SET ANY_CS)
RETURN NATURAL;
```

Returns the length of string *ch*.

```
FUNCTION LENGTHB
    (ch IN VARCHAR2 CHARACTER SET ANY_CS)
RETURN NUMBER;
```

Returns the length in bytes of *ch*.

```
FUNCTION LOWER
    (ch IN VARCHAR2 CHARACTER SET ANY_CS)
RETURN VARCHAR2;
```

Returns *ch* with all characters in lowercase.

```
FUNCTION LPAD
    (str1 IN VARCHAR2 CHARACTER SET ANY_CS
    ,len BINARY_INTEGER
[,pad IN VARCHAR2 CHARACTER SET str1%CHARSET])
RETURN VARCHAR2;
```

Returns *str1* padded on the left to a length of *len* with pad
character *pad*.

```
FUNCTION LTRIM
    (str1 IN VARCHAR2 CHARACTER SET ANY_CS := ' '
[,tset IN VARCHAR2 CHARACTER SET str1%CHARSET])
RETURN VARCHAR2;
```

Returns *str1* stripped of any leading characters that appear
in *tset*.

```
FUNCTION REPLACE
    (srcstr IN VARCHAR2 CHARACTER SET ANY_CS
    ,oldsub IN VARCHAR2 CHARACTER SET srcstr%CHARSET
    ,newsub IN VARCHAR2 CHARACTER SET
        srcstr%CHARSET:= NULL)
RETURN VARCHAR2;
```

Returns *scrstr* with all occurrences of *oldsub* replaced with *newsub*.

```
FUNCTION RPAD
    (str1 IN VARCHAR2 CHARACTER SET ANY_CS
    ,len BINARY_INTEGER
[,pad IN VARCHAR2 CHARACTER SET str1%CHARSET])
RETURN VARCHAR2;
```

Returns *str1* padded on the right to a length of *len* using pad character *pad*.

```
FUNCTION RTRIM
    (str1 IN VARCHAR2 CHARACTER SET ANY_CS := ' '
[,tset IN VARCHAR2 CHARACTER SET str1%CHARSET])
RETURN VARCHAR2;
```

Returns *str1* stripped of any trailing characters that appear in *tset*.

```
FUNCTION SOUNDEX
    (ch IN VARCHAR2 CHARACTER SET ANY_CS)
RETURN VARCHAR2;
```

Returns the soundex (phonetic) encoding of *ch*.

```
FUNCTION SUBSTR
    (str1 IN VARCHAR2 CHARACTER SET ANY_CS
    ,pos BINARY_INTEGER
    ,len BINARY_INTEGER := NULL)
RETURN VARCHAR2;
```

Returns the portion of *str1* beginning *pos* characters into *str1* and extending for *len* characters. Negatives in *pos* or *len* cause the positions to be counted from right to left (backwards).

```
FUNCTION SUBSTRB
    (str1 IN VARCHAR2 CHARACTER SET ANY_CS
    ,pos BINARY_INTEGER
    ,len BINARY_INTEGER := NULL)
RETURN VARCHAR2;
```

Same as SUBSTR except *pos* and *len* are expressed in bytes (for multi-byte character sets).

```
FUNCTION TRANSLATE
    (str1 IN VARCHAR2 CHARACTER SET ANY_CS
    ,src IN VARCHAR2 CHARACTER SET str1%CHARSET
    ,dest IN VARCHAR2 CHARACTER SET str1%CHARSET)
RETURN VARCHAR2;
```

Returns *str1* with all occurrences of characters in *src* replaced by positionally corresponding characters in *dest*.

```
FUNCTION UPPER
    (ch IN VARCHAR2 CHARACTER SET ANY_CS)
RETURN VARCHAR2;
```

Returns the string *ch* in all uppercase.

Numeric Functions

Numeric functions manipulate numbers.

```
FUNCTION ABS (n IN NUMBER) RETURN NUMBER;
```

Returns the absolute value of *n*.

```
FUNCTION ACOS (n IN NUMBER) RETURN NUMBER;
```

Returns the arc cosine of *n* where $-1 < n < 1$.

```
FUNCTION ASIN (n IN NUMBER) RETURN NUMBER;
```

Returns the arc sine of *n* where $-1 < n < 1$.

```
FUNCTION ATAN (n IN NUMBER) RETURN NUMBER;
```

Returns the inverse tangent of *n*.

```
FUNCTION ATAN2
    (x IN NUMBER, y IN NUMBER)
RETURN NUMBER;
```

Returns the arc tangent of *x* and *y*.

```
FUNCTION CEIL (n IN NUMBER) RETURN NUMBER;
```

Returns the nearest integer greater than or equal to *n*.

```
FUNCTION COS (n IN NUMBER) RETURN NUMBER;
```

Returns the trigonometric cosine of *n*.

```
FUNCTION COSH (n IN NUMBER) RETURN NUMBER;
```

Returns the hyperbolic cosine of *n*.

```
FUNCTION EXP (n IN NUMBER) RETURN NUMBER;
```

Returns the value of *e* raised to the *n*th power where *e* is the base of the natural logarithms.

```
FUNCTION FLOOR (n IN NUMBER) RETURN NUMBER;
```
Returns the nearest integer less than or equal to *n*.

```
FUNCTION LN (n IN NUMBER) RETURN NUMBER;
```
Returns the natural logarithm of *n*.

```
FUNCTION LOG
    (left IN NUMBER, right IN NUMBER)
RETURN NUMBER;
```
Returns the logarithm of *right* in base *left* where *left* >1
and *right* >0.

```
FUNCTION MOD
    (n1 IN NUMBER, n2 IN NUMBER)
RETURN NUMBER;
```
Returns the remainder of *n1* after division by *n2*.

```
FUNCTION POWER
    (n IN NUMBER, e IN NUMBER)
RETURN NUMBER;
```
Returns *n* raised to the *e*th power.

```
FUNCTION ROUND
    (left IN NUMBER
    ,right BINARY_INTEGER := 0)
RETURN NUMBER;
```
Returns *left* rounded to *right* decimal places.

```
FUNCTION SIGN (n IN NUMBER) RETURN SIGNTYPE;
```
Returns -1, 0, or 1, depending on the sign of *n*.

```
FUNCTION SIN (n IN NUMBER) RETURN NUMBER;
```
Returns the trigonometric sine function of *n*.

```
FUNCTION SINH (n IN NUMBER) RETURN NUMBER;
```
Returns the hyperbolic sine of *n*.

```
FUNCTION SQRT (n IN NUMBER) RETURN NUMBER;
```
Returns the square root of *n*.

```
FUNCTION TAN (n IN NUMBER) RETURN NUMBER;
```
Returns the trigonometric tangent function of *n*.

```
FUNCTION TANH (n IN NUMBER) RETURN NUMBER;
```

Returns the hyperbolic tangent of *n*.

```
FUNCTION TRUNC
    (n IN NUMBER
    ,places BINARY_INTEGER := 0)
RETURN NUMBER;
```

Truncates *n* to *places* decimal places.

Date Functions

Date functions manipulate date information.

```
FUNCTION ADD_MONTHS
    (left IN DATE | NUMBER
    ,right IN NUMBER | DATE)
RETURN DATE;
```

Returns the date resulting from adding right months to the *left* date.

```
FUNCTION LAST_DAY (right IN DATE) RETURN DATE;
```

Returns the last day of the month containing date *right*.

```
FUNCTION MONTHS_BETWEEN
    (left IN DATE, right IN DATE)
RETURN NUMBER;
```

Returns the number of months between *left* and *right*.

```
FUNCTION NEW_TIME
    (right IN DATE
    ,middle IN VARCHAR2
    ,left IN VARCHAR2)
RETURN DATE;
```

Returns the date when date *right* is converted from time zone *middle* to time zone *left*.

```
FUNCTION NEXT_DAY
    (left IN DATE, right IN VARCHAR2)
RETURN DATE;
```

Returns the next occurrence of day of the week *right* ("Monday", "Tuesday", etc.) after date *left*.

```
FUNCTION ROUND
    (left IN DATE [,right IN VARCHAR2])
RETURN DATE;
```

Returns date *left* rounded according to format mask *right* (or the default format DD).

```
FUNCTION SYSDATE RETURN DATE;
```

Returns the current system date from the database.

```
FUNCTION TRUNC
    (left IN DATE [,right IN VARCHAR2])
RETURN DATE;
```

Returns the date *left* truncated using format mask *right* (or the default format DD).

Conversion Functions

Conversion functions convert data to the right datatype for an operation.

```
FUNCTION CHARTOROWID (str IN VARCHAR2) RETURN ROWID;
```

Returns *str* converted from VARCHAR2 to the ROWID datatype. See also DBMS_ROWID.

```
FUNCTION CONVERT
    (src IN VARCHAR2
    ,destcset IN VARCHAR2
    [,srccset IN VARCHAR2])
RETURN VARCHAR2;
```

Returns *src* converted from character set *srcset* to *destcset*. The default for *srccset* is the database's default character set.

```
FUNCTION HEXTORAW (c IN VARCHAR2) RETURN RAW;
```

Returns the hexadecimal encoded VARCHAR *c* as a RAW string.

```
FUNCTION RAWTOHEX (r IN RAW) RETURN VARCHAR2;
```

Returns the RAW string *r* as a hexadecimal encoded VARCHAR.

```
FUNCTION ROWIDTOCHAR (str IN ROWID) RETURN VARCHAR2;
```

Returns the ROWID data in *str* converted to a VARCHAR.

```
FUNCTION TO_CHAR
    (left IN DATE | NUMBER
    [,right IN VARCHAR2])
    [,parms IN VARCHAR2])
RETURN VARCHAR2;
```

Returns *left* converted from a NUMBER or DATE to a
VARCHAR, using format mask *right* if specified. The
optional *parms* can specify NLS language parameters.

```
FUNCTION TO_DATE
    (left IN VARCHAR2 | NUMBER
    [,right IN VARCHAR2]
    [,parms IN VARCHAR2])
RETURN DATE;
```

Returns *left* converted from a NUMBER or VARCHAR to a
DATE, using format mask *right* if specified. The optional
parms can specify NLS language parameters.

```
FUNCTION TO_NUMBER
    (left IN VARCHAR2 | NUMBER
    [,right IN VARCHAR2]
    [,parms IN VARCHAR2])
RETURN NUMBER;
```

Returns *left* converted from a VARCHAR or NUMBER to a
DATE, using format mask *right* if specified. The optional
parms can specify NLS language parameters.

LOB Functions

LOB functions initialize large object (LOB) values.

```
FUNCTION BFILENAME
    (directory IN VARCHAR2
    ,filename IN VARCHAR2)
RETURN BFILE;
```

Returns a BFILE locator (handle) to *filename* in directory
directory. See also DBMS_LOB.

```
FUNCTION EMPTY_BLOB RETURN BLOB;
```

Returns an empty locator of type BLOB.

```
FUNCTION EMPTY_CLOB RETURN CLOB;
```

Returns an empty locator of type CLOB.

Miscellaneous Functions

Miscellaneous functions return a variety of useful information.

```
FUNCTION BITAND
    (left BINARY_INTEGER
    ,right BINARY_INTEGER)
RETURN BINARY_INTEGER;
```

Returns the bitwise AND of *left* and *right*.

```
FUNCTION DUMP
    (e IN NUMBER | DATE | VARCHAR2
    ,df BINARY_INTEGER := NULL
    ,sp BINARY_INTEGER := NULL
    ,len BINARY_INTEGER := NULL)
RETURN VARCHAR2;
```

Returns the internal representation of the portion of *e* starting at *sp* of length *len* and using dump format *df* (8 = octal; 10 = decimal; 16 = hex; 17 = char).

```
FUNCTION GREATEST
    (pattern IN NUMBER | VARCHAR | DATE)
RETURN NUMBER | VARCHAR | DATE;
```

Returns the greatest value of the (two or more) expressions listed in *pattern. pattern* expressions must all have the same datatype.

```
FUNCTION LEAST
    (pattern IN NUMBER | VARCHAR | DATE)
RETURN NUMBER | VARCHAR | DATE;
```

Returns the smallest value of the (two or more) expressions listed in *pattern. pattern* is a comma-delimited list of expressions that all have the same datatype.

```
FUNCTION NVL
    (s1 | n1 | d1 | b1  IN VARCHAR2 | NUMBER | DATE |
        BOOLEAN
    ,s2 | n2 | d2 | b2 IN VARCHAR2 CHARACTER SET
        s1%CHARSET)
RETURN VARCHAR2 | NUMBER | DATE | BOOLEAN;
```

NULL value function; returns *s2 | n2 | d2 | b2* when *s1 | n1 | d1 | b1* is NULL, otherwise *s1 | n1 | d1 | b1.*

```
FUNCTION SQLCODE RETURN NUMBER;
```

Returns the numeric code associated with the current
execution status.

```
FUNCTION SQLERRM [(code IN NUMBER)] RETURN VARCHAR2;
```

Returns the error message associated with *code* (or the
current SQLCODE by default).

```
FUNCTION UID RETURN NUMBER;
```

Returns the numeric user id of the current user.

```
FUNCTION USER RETURN VARCHAR2;
```

Returns the character username of the current user.

```
FUNCTION USERENV (envstr IN VARCHAR2) RETURN VARCHAR2;
```

Returns the user session environment information specified by *envstr*, which can have the following values:

ENTRYID

To return an auditing identifier.

INSTANCE

To return the instance identifier for an OPS database.

LANGUAGE

To return NLS settings (language, territory, and character set) for the session.

TERMINAL

To return the operating system terminal identifier.

```
FUNCTION VSIZE
   (e IN NUMBER | DATE | VARCHAR2)
RETURN NUMBER;
```

Returns the number of bytes used to store *e* internally.

```
FUNCTION XOR
   (left IN BOOLEAN, right IN BOOLEAN)
RETURN BOOLEAN;
```

Returns TRUE when either *left* or *right* is TRUE but not
both. See also UTL_RAW.

RESTRICT REFERENCES
Pragmas

A pragma is a directive to the PL/SQL compiler. Pragmas pass information to the compiler; they are processed at compile time but do not execute. If you include a call to a built-in package in a SQL statement, you must include a RESTRICT REFERENCES pragma in your code. This pragma tells the compiler the purity level (freedom from side effects) of a packaged program. The purity levels available are:

- WNDS—Writes no database state
- RNDS—Reads no database state
- WNPS—Writes no package state
- RNPS—Reads no package state

DBMS_LOB Programs	WNDS	RNDS	WNPS	RNPS
COMPARE	✓	✓	✓	✓
FILEEXISTS	✓	✓	✓	✓
FILEISOPEN	✓	✓	✓	✓
GETLENGTH	✓	✓	✓	✓
INSTR	✓	✓	✓	✓
SUBSTR	✓	✓	✓	✓

DBMS_OUTPUT Programs	WNDS	RNDS	WNPS	RNPS
DISABLE	✓	✓		
ENABLE	✓	✓		
GET_LINE	✓	✓		
GET_LINES	✓	✓		
NEW_LINE	✓	✓		
PUT	✓	✓		
PUT_LINE	✓	✓		

DBMS_PIPE Programs	WNDS	RNDS	WNPS	RNPS
CREATE_PIPE	✓	✓		
NEXT_ITEM_TYPE	✓	✓		
PACK_MESSAGE	✓	✓		
PACK_MESSAGE_RAW	✓	✓		
PACK_MESSAGE_ROWID	✓	✓		
PURGE	✓	✓		
RECEIVE_MESSAGE	✓	✓		
REMOVE_PIPE	✓	✓		
RESET_BUFFER	✓	✓		
SEND_MESSAGE	✓	✓		
UNIQUE_SESSION_NAME	✓	✓	✓	
UNPACK_MESSAGE	✓	✓		
UNPACK_MESSAGE_RAW	✓	✓		
UNPACK_MESSAGE_ROWID	✓	✓		

DBMS_ROWID Programs	WNDS	RNDS	WNPS	RNPS
ROWID_BLOCK_NUMBER	✓	✓	✓	✓
ROWID_CREATE	✓	✓	✓	✓
ROWID_INFO	✓	✓	✓	✓
ROWID_OBJECT	✓	✓	✓	✓
ROWID_RELATIVE_FNO	✓	✓	✓	✓
ROWID_ROW_NUMBER	✓	✓	✓	✓
ROWID_TO_ABSOLUTE_FNO	✓		✓	✓
ROWID_TO_EXTENDED	✓		✓	✓
ROWID_TO_RESTRICTED	✓	✓	✓	✓
ROWID_TYPE	✓	✓	✓	✓
ROWID_VERIFY	✓		✓	✓

DBMS_SESSION Program	WNDS	RNDS	WNPS	RNPS
UNIQUE_SESSION_ID	✓	✓	✓	

DBMS_SQL Programs	WNDS	RNDS	WNPS	RNPS
BIND_ARRAY	✓			
BIND_VARIABLE	✓			
BIND_VARIABLE_CHAR	✓			
BIND_VARIABLE_RAW	✓			
BIND_VARIABLE_ROWID	✓			
CLOSE_CURSOR	✓	✓		
COLUMN_VALUE	✓	✓		
COLUMN_VALUE_CHAR	✓	✓		
COLUMN_VALUE_LONG	✓	✓		
COLUMN_VALUE_RAW	✓	✓		
COLUMN_VALUE_ROWID	✓	✓		
DEFINE_ARRAY	✓	✓		
DEFINE_COLUMN	✓	✓		
DEFINE_COLUMN_CHAR	✓	✓		
DEFINE_COLUMN_LONG	✓	✓		
DEFINE_COLUMN_RAW	✓	✓		
DEFINE_COLUMN_ROWID	✓	✓		
DESCRIBE_COLUMNS	✓			
EXECUTE_AND_FETCH	✓			
FETCH_ROWS	✓			
IS_OPEN	✓	✓		
LAST_ERROR_POSITION	✓	✓		
LAST_ROW_COUNT	✓	✓		
LAST_ROW_ID	✓	✓		
LAST_SQL_FUNCTION_CODE	✓	✓		
OPEN_CURSOR	✓	✓		

DBMS_SQL Programs	WNDS	RNDS	WNPS	RNPS
VARIABLE_VALUE	✓	✓		
VARIABLE_VALUE_CHAR	✓	✓		
VARIABLE_VALUE_RAW	✓	✓		
VARIABLE_VALUE_ROWID	✓	✓		

DBMS_STANDARD Programs	WNDS	RNDS	WNPS	RNPS
DELETING	✓		✓	✓
INSERTING	✓		✓	✓
RAISE_APPLICATION_ERROR	✓	✓	✓	✓
UPDATING	✓		✓	✓

DBMS_UTILITY Programs	WNDS	RNDS	WNPS	RNPS
DATA_BLOCK_ADDRESS_BLOCK	✓	✓	✓	✓
DATA_BLOCK_ADDRESS_FILE	✓	✓	✓	✓
GET_HASH_VALUE	✓	✓	✓	✓
MAKE_DATA_BLOCK_ADDRESS	✓	✓	✓	✓
PORT_STRING	✓	✓	✓	✓

UTL_RAW Programs	WNDS	RNDS	WNPS	RNPS
BIT_AND	✓	✓	✓	✓
BIT_COMPLEMENT	✓	✓	✓	✓
BIT_OR	✓	✓	✓	✓
BIT_XOR	✓	✓	✓	✓
CAST_TO_RAW	✓	✓	✓	✓
CAST_TO_VARCHAR2	✓	✓	✓	✓
COMPARE	✓	✓	✓	✓
CONCAT	✓	✓	✓	✓

UTL_RAW Programs	WNDS	RNDS	WNPS	RNPS
CONVERT	✓	✓	✓	✓
COPIES	✓	✓	✓	✓
LENGTH	✓	✓	✓	✓
OVERLAY	✓	✓	✓	✓
REVERSE	✓	✓	✓	✓
SUBSTR	✓	✓	✓	✓
TRANSLATE	✓	✓	✓	✓
TRANSLITERATE	✓	✓	✓	✓
XRANGE	✓	✓	✓	✓

Nonprogram Elements

In addition to the definitions for the programs (shown earlier in the "Built-in Packages" section), a package specification may contain nonprogram elements defined for that package. These elements may include constants, exceptions, record types, and index-by tables.

This section shows the nonprogram elements defined for each of the built-in packages.

DBMS_ALERT

```
maxwait CONSTANT INTEGER := 86400000;
```

DBMS_APPLICATION_INFO

```
set_session_longops_nohint
  CONSTANT BINARY_INTEGER := -1;
```

DBMS_AQ

```
before          CONSTANT BINARY_INTEGER
browse          CONSTANT BINARY_INTEGER
expired         CONSTANT BINARY_INTEGER
first_message   CONSTANT BINARY_INTEGER
forever         CONSTANT BINARY_INTEGER
immediate       CONSTANT BINARY_INTEGER
locked          CONSTANT BINARY_INTEGER
```

```
never               CONSTANT  BINARY_INTEGER
next_message        CONSTANT  BINARY_INTEGER
next_transaction    CONSTANT  BINARY_INTEGER
no_delay            CONSTANT  BINARY_INTEGER
no_wait             CONSTANT  BINARY_INTEGER
on_commit           CONSTANT  BINARY_INTEGER
processed           CONSTANT  BINARY_INTEGER
ready               CONSTANT  BINARY_INTEGER
remove              CONSTANT  BINARY_INTEGER
top                 CONSTANT  BINARY_INTEGER
waiting             CONSTANT  BINARY_INTEGER


TYPE aq$_recipient_list_t IS TABLE OF sys.aq$_agent
  INDEX BY BINARY_INTEGER;

TYPE message_properties_t IS RECORD
   (priority         BINARY_INTEGER DEFAULT 1
   ,delay            BINARY_INTEGER
                        DEFAULT DBMS_AQ.no_delay
   ,expiration       BINARY_INTEGER
                        DEFAULT DBMS_AQ.never
   ,correlation      VARCHAR2(128) DEFAULT NULL
   ,attempts         BINARY_INTEGER
   ,recipient_list   DBMS_AQ.aq$_recipient_list_t
   ,exception_queue  VARCHAR2(51) DEFAULT NULL
   ,enqueue_time     DATE
   ,state            BINARY_INTEGER);

TYPE enqueue_options_t IS RECORD
   (visibility          BINARY_INTEGER
                        DEFAULT DBMS_AQ.on_commit
   ,relative_msgid      RAW(16) DEFAULT NULL
   ,sequence_deviation BINARY_INTEGER DEFAULT NULL);

TYPE dequeue_options_t IS RECORD
   (consumer_name  VARCHAR2(30) DEFAULT NULL
   ,dequeue_mode   BINARY_INTEGER
                        DEFAULT DBMS_AQ.remove
   ,navigation     BINARY_INTEGER
                        DEFAULT DBMS_AQ.next_message
   ,visibility     BINARY_INTEGER
                        DEFAULT DBMS_AQ.on_commit
   ,wait           BINARY_INTEGER
                        DEFAULT DBMS_AQ.forever
   ,msgid          RAW(16) DEFAULT NULL
   ,correlation    VARCHAR2(128) DEFAULT NULL);
```

DBMS_AQADM

```
exception_queue CONSTANT BINARY_INTEGER := 1;
infinite        CONSTANT BINARY_INTEGER := -1;
none            CONSTANT BINARY_INTEGER := 0;
normal_queue    CONSTANT BINARY_INTEGER := 0;
transactional   CONSTANT BINARY_INTEGER := 1;

TYPE aq$_subscriber_list_t IS TABLE OF sys.aq$_agent
   INDEX BY BINARY_INTEGER;
```

DBMS_DESCRIBE

```
TYPE varchar2_table IS TABLE OF VARCHAR2(30)
   INDEX BY BINARY_INTEGER;

TYPE number_table IS TABLE OF NUMBER
   INDEX BY BINARY_INTEGER;
```

DBMS_LOB

```
invalid_argval EXCEPTION;
PRAGMA EXCEPTION_INIT(invalid_argval, -21560);

access_error EXCEPTION;
PRAGMA EXCEPTION_INIT(access_error, -22925);

noexist_directory EXCEPTION;
PRAGMA EXCEPTION_INIT(noexist_directory, -22285);

nopriv_directory EXCEPTION;
PRAGMA EXCEPTION_INIT(nopriv_directory, -22286);

invalid_directory EXCEPTION;
PRAGMA EXCEPTION_INIT(invalid_directory, -22287);

operation_failed EXCEPTION;
PRAGMA EXCEPTION_INIT(operation_failed, -22288);

unopened_file EXCEPTION;
PRAGMA EXCEPTION_INIT(unopened_file, -22289);

open_toomany EXCEPTION;
PRAGMA EXCEPTION_INIT(open_toomany, -22290);

file_readonly CONSTANT BINARY_INTEGER := 0;
lobmaxsize    CONSTANT INTEGER := 4294967295;
```

```
invalid_argval_num        NUMBER := 21560;
access_error_num          NUMBER := 22925;
noexist_directory_num     NUMBER := 22285;
nopriv_directory_num      NUMBER := 22286;
invalid_directory_num     NUMBER := 22287;
operation_failed_num      NUMBER := 22288;
unopened_file_num         NUMBER := 22289;
open_toomany_num          NUMBER := 22290;
```

DBMS_LOCK

```
nl_mode   CONSTANT INTEGER := 1;
ss_mode   CONSTANT INTEGER := 2;
sx_mode   CONSTANT INTEGER := 3;
s_mode    CONSTANT INTEGER := 4;
ssx_mode  CONSTANT INTEGER := 5;
x_mode    CONSTANT INTEGER := 6;
maxwait   CONSTANT INTEGER := 32767;
```

DBMS_OUTPUT

```
TYPE chararr IS TABLE OF VARCHAR2(255)
  INDEX BY BINARY_INTEGER;
```

DBMS_PIPE

```
maxwait CONSTANT INTEGER := 86400000;
```

DBMS_ROWID

```
rowid_invalid EXCEPTION;
PRAGMA EXCEPTION_INIT(rowid_invalid, -1410);

rowid_bad_block EXCEPTION;
PRAGMA EXCEPTION_INIT(rowid_bad_block, -28516);

rowid_convert_external CONSTANT INTEGER := 1;
rowid_convert_internal CONSTANT INTEGER := 0;
rowid_is_invalid       CONSTANT INTEGER := 1;
rowid_is_valid         CONSTANT INTEGER := 0;
rowid_object_undefined CONSTANT INTEGER := 0;
rowid_type_extended    CONSTANT INTEGER := 1;
rowid_type_restricted  CONSTANT INTEGER := 0;
```

DBMS_SQL

```
inconsistent_type EXCEPTION;
PRAGMA EXCEPTION_INIT(inconsistent_type, -6562);

v6      CONSTANT INTEGER := 0;
native CONSTANT INTEGER := 1;
v7      CONSTANT INTEGER := 2;

TYPE varchar2s IS TABLE OF VARCHAR2(256)
  INDEX BY BINARY_INTEGER;

TYPE desc_rec IS RECORD
  (col_type BINARY_INTEGER := 0
  ,col_max_len BINARY_INTEGER := 0
  ,col_name varchar2(32) := ''
  ,col_name_len BINARY_INTEGER := 0
  ,col_schema_name VARCHAR2(32) := ''
  ,col_schema_name_len BINARY_INTEGER := 0
  ,col_precision BINARY_INTEGER := 0
  ,col_scale BINARY_INTEGER := 0
  ,col_charsetid BINARY_INTEGER := 0
  ,col_charsetform BINARY_INTEGER := 0
  ,col_null_ok BOOLEAN := TRUE);

TYPE desc_tab IS TABLE OF desc_rec
  INDEX BY BINARY_INTEGER;

TYPE number_table IS TABLE OF NUMBER
  INDEX BY BINARY_INTEGER;

TYPE varchar2_table IS TABLE OF VARCHAR2(2000)
  INDEX BY BINARY_INTEGER;

TYPE date_table IS TABLE OF DATE
  INDEX BY BINARY_INTEGER;

TYPE blob_table IS TABLE OF BLOB
  INDEX BY BINARY_INTEGER;

TYPE clob_table IS TABLE OF CLOB
  INDEX BY BINARY_INTEGER;

TYPE bfile_table IS TABLE OF BFILE
  INDEX BY BINARY_INTEGER;
```

DBMS_TRANSACTION

```
discrete_transaction_failed EXCEPTION;
PRAGMA EXCEPTION_INIT(discrete_transaction_failed,
    -8175);

consistent_read_failure EXCEPTION;
PRAGMA EXCEPTION_INIT(consistent_read_failure, -8176);
```

DBMS_UTILITY

```
TYPE uncl_array IS TABLE OF VARCHAR2(227)
  INDEX BY BINARY_INTEGER;

TYPE name_array IS TABLE OF VARCHAR2(30)
  INDEX BY BINARY_INTEGER;

TYPE dblink_array IS TABLE OF VARCHAR2(128)
  INDEX BY BINARY_INTEGER;

TYPE index_table_type IS TABLE OF BINARY_INTEGER
  INDEX BY BINARY_INTEGER;

TYPE number_array IS TABLE OF NUMBER
  INDEX BY BINARY_INTEGER;
```

UTL_FILE

```
internal_error EXCEPTION;
invalid_filehandle EXCEPTION;
invalid_mode EXCEPTION;
invalid_operation EXCEPTION;
invalid_path EXCEPTION;
read_error EXCEPTION;
write_error EXCEPTION;

TYPE file_type IS RECORD (id BINARY_INTEGER);
```

STANDARD

Following are the nonprogram elements for the STANDARD package.

Exceptions

```
dup_val_on_index EXCEPTION;
PRAGMA EXCEPTION_INIT(dup_val_on_index, '-0001');

timeout_on_resource EXCEPTION;
PRAGMA EXCEPTION_INIT(timeout_on_resource, '-0051');

invalid_cursor EXCEPTION;
PRAGMA EXCEPTION_INIT(invalid_cursor, '-1001');

not_logged_on EXCEPTION;
PRAGMA EXCEPTION_INIT(not_logged_on, '-1012');

login_denied EXCEPTION;
PRAGMA EXCEPTION_INIT(login_denied, '-1017');

too_many_rows EXCEPTION;
PRAGMA EXCEPTION_INIT(too_many_rows, '-1422');

zero_divide EXCEPTION;
PRAGMA EXCEPTION_INIT(zero_divide, '-1476');

invalid_number EXCEPTION;
PRAGMA EXCEPTION_INIT(invalid_number, '-1722');

storage_error EXCEPTION;
PRAGMA EXCEPTION_INIT(storage_error, '-6500');

program_error EXCEPTION;
PRAGMA EXCEPTION_INIT(program_error, '-6501');

value_error EXCEPTION;
PRAGMA EXCEPTION_INIT(value_error, '-6502');

rowtype_mismatch EXCEPTION;
PRAGMA EXCEPTION_INIT(rowtype_mismatch, '-6504');

cursor_already_open EXCEPTION;
PRAGMA EXCEPTION_INIT(cursor_already_open, '-6511');

access_into_null EXCEPTION;
PRAGMA EXCEPTION_INIT(access_into_null, '-6530');

collection_is_null EXCEPTION;
PRAGMA EXCEPTION_INIT(collection_is_null , '-6531');
```

```
subscript_outside_limit EXCEPTION;
PRAGMA EXCEPTION_INIT(subscript_outside_limit,'-6532');

subscript_beyond_count EXCEPTION;
PRAGMA EXCEPTION_INIT(subscript_beyond_count ,'-6533');

no_data_found EXCEPTION;
PRAGMA EXCEPTION_INIT(no_data_found, 100);
```

Numeric datatypes

```
TYPE NUMBER IS NUMBER_BASE;
SUBTYPE BINARY_INTEGER IS INTEGER RANGE '-
    2147483647'..2147483647;
SUBTYPE CURSOR_HANDLE IS BINARY_INTEGER RANGE 0..255;
SUBTYPE DEC IS DECIMAL;
SUBTYPE DECIMAL IS NUMBER(38,0);
SUBTYPE "DOUBLE PRECISION" IS FLOAT;
SUBTYPE FLOAT IS NUMBER; -- NUMBER(126)
SUBTYPE INT IS INTEGER;
SUBTYPE INTEGER IS NUMBER(38,0);
SUBTYPE NATURAL IS BINARY_INTEGER RANGE 0..2147483647;
SUBTYPE NATURALN IS NATURAL NOT NULL;
SUBTYPE NUMERIC IS DECIMAL;
SUBTYPE PLS_INTEGER IS BINARY_INTEGER;
SUBTYPE POSITIVE IS BINARY_INTEGER RANGE
    1..2147483647;
SUBTYPE POSITIVEN IS POSITIVE NOT NULL;
SUBTYPE REAL IS FLOAT; -- FLOAT(63)
SUBTYPE SIGNTYPE IS BINARY_INTEGER RANGE '-1'..1;  --
    for SIGN functions
SUBTYPE SMALLINT IS NUMBER(38,0);
```

Character datatypes

```
TYPE VARCHAR2 IS NEW CHAR_BASE;
SUBTYPE CHAR IS VARCHAR2;
SUBTYPE CHARACTER IS CHAR;
SUBTYPE "CHAR VARYING" IS VARCHAR;
SUBTYPE "CHARACTER VARYING" IS VARCHAR;
SUBTYPE LONG IS VARCHAR2(32760);
SUBTYPE "LONG RAW" IS RAW(32760);
SUBTYPE RAW IS VARCHAR2;
SUBTYPE ROWID IS VARCHAR2(256);
SUBTYPE STRING IS VARCHAR2;
SUBTYPE VARCHAR IS VARCHAR2;
```

```
SUBTYPE "NCHAR" IS CHAR CHARACTER SET NCHAR_CS;
SUBTYPE "NCHAR VARYING" IS VARCHAR CHARACTER SET
    NCHAR_CS;
SUBTYPE "NCLOB" IS CLOB CHARACTER SET NCHAR_CS;
SUBTYPE "NVARCHAR2" IS VARCHAR2 CHARACTER SET NCHAR_CS;
SUBTYPE "NATIONAL CHAR VARYING" IS
    VARCHAR CHARACTER SET NCHAR_CS;
SUBTYPE "NATIONAL CHAR" IS CHAR CHARACTER SET NCHAR_CS;
SUBTYPE "NATIONAL CHARACTER LARGE OBJECT" IS
    CLOB CHARACTER SET NCHAR_CS;
SUBTYPE "NATIONAL CHARACTER VARYING" IS
    VARCHAR CHARACTER SET NCHAR_CS;
SUBTYPE "NATIONAL CHARACTER" IS
    CHAR CHARACTER SET NCHAR_CS;
SUBTYPE "NCHAR LARGE OBJECT" IS
    CLOB CHARACTER SET NCHAR_CS;
```

LOB datatypes

```
TYPE BFILE IS BFILE_BASE;
TYPE BLOB IS BLOB_BASE;
TYPE CLOB IS CLOB_BASE;
SUBTYPE "BINARY LARGE OBJECT" IS BLOB;
SUBTYPE "CHAR LARGE OBJECT" IS CLOB;
SUBTYPE "CHARACTER LARGE OBJECT" IS CLOB;
```

Other datatypes

```
TYPE BOOLEAN IS (FALSE, TRUE);
TYPE DATE IS DATE_BASE;
TYPE MLSLABEL IS NEW CHAR_BASE;
```

Web Programming

Dynamic HTML:
The Definitive Reference

By Danny Goodman
1st Edition July 1998
1088 pages, ISBN 1-56592-494-0

WebMaster in a Nutshell

By Stephen Spainhour & Valerie Quercia
1st Edition October 1996
374 pages, ISBN 1-56592-229-8

WebMaster in a Nutshell,
Deluxe Edition

By O'Reilly & Associates, Inc.
1st Edition September 1997
374 pages, includes CD-ROM & book
ISBN 1-56592-305-7

HTML: The Definitive Guide,
2nd Edition

By Chuck Musciano & Bill Kennedy
2nd Edition May 1997
552 pages, ISBN 1-56592-235-2

Frontier: The Definitive Guide

By Matt Neuburg
1st Edition February 1998
618 pages, 1-56592-383-9

Learning VBScript

By Paul Lomax
1st Edition July 1997
616 pages, includes CD-ROM
ISBN 1-56592-247-6

CGI Programming on
the World Wide Web

By Shishir Gundavaram
1st Edition March 1996
450 pages, ISBN 1-56592-168-2

JavaScript: The Definitive Guide,
3rd Edition

By David Flanagan & Dan Shafer
3rd Edition June 1998
800 pages, ISBN 1-56592-392-8

Web Client Programming
with Perl

By Clinton Wong
1st Edition March 1997
228 pages, ISBN 1-56592-214-X

Information Architecture
for the World Wide Web

By Louis Rosenfeld & Peter Morville
1st Edition January 1998
226 pages, ISBN 1-56592-282-4